BONNARD

Annette Vaillant

WITH A DIALOGUE BETWEEN
JEAN CASSOU AND RAYMOND COGNIAT

COMMENTARIES BY HANS R. HAHNLOSER

NEW YORK GRAPHIC SOCIETY
Greenwich, Connecticut

TRANSLATED FROM THE FRENCH
BY DAVID BRITT

Library of Congress Catalogue Card Number 66 - 15 800
© 1965 Editions Ides et Calendes, Neuchâtel, Switzerland
Printed in Switzerland
Reproduction rights reserved by SPADEM and ADAGP, Paris

CONTENTS

DIALOGUE BETWEEN RAYMOND COGNIAT
AND JEAN CASSOU

RAYMOND COGNIAT I only met Bonnard a few times, and when we did meet our mutual shyness prevented any real exchange of ideas. From a human point of view, I regret having missed a precious opportunity, but I do not think that I understand his art any less well than if I had known the man. On the contrary, the freedom from anecdote makes it possible to see the work more clearly as a whole, as if it belonged to the distant past.

To some extent, I think it is harder to judge the work of an artist if one knows him intimately. One's feelings about the artist cloud and distort one's vision of what he creates. I prefer to see Bonnard's work impersonally, as a whole —but I am sorry for other reasons that I had no chance to enjoy the friendship of a man who had such good friends as Bonnard had.

JEAN CASSOU It is true that knowing any artist adds an extra dimension to our appreciation of his work. But, although contact with living artists is such an enriching experience, it is no bad thing if, in our youth, we know the painting before we know the painter.

RAYMOND COGNIAT This happened to me with Bonnard. His work was my initiation into modern art. It is impossible to exaggerate the impression this made on me. For the first time I doubted the universal validity of the traditional principles I had hitherto accepted without question. And for the first time I realized that non-conformism was not incompatible with seriousness and sincerity. In those far-off days I still had no idea of what looking at a picture could lead to.

The year was 1912. Outside the Galerie Bernheim-Jeune, on the Boulevard de la Madeleine, a poster invited the curious passer-by to visit an exhibition of the works of Pierre Bonnard. Entry free. Why not go in and see? I was a very young man, rather lost in the austere although not unfriendly silence of the gallery. How could such a dignified setting house such disquieting pictures? In those days, anything which did not tend towards photographic realism seemed disquieting to me. It couldn't be somebody's whimsy, still less a trick; in a place like this it was unthinkable. But how could anyone expect to sell these intimate scenes, observed as they were from such an original angle, with such unexpected effects of perspective and foreshortening, such unaccustomed harmonies of colour? Who would buy them?

This was a mystery; a door opened on a new and enigmatic realm. I was beginning to see that life contains a certain number of question-marks; I was tempted to look for an explanation. I did not realize it at the time, but, thanks to Bonnard, I was taking my first steps as a lover

of art and as a critic. I decided to approach the problem with as much good-will as I could, trying to comprehend rather than reject, to experience rather than to argue.

I remember that first encounter because, in spite of my surprise, I was affected by the charm, I might almost say the enchantment, of these works.

Such a direct impression is unforgettable. I don't think there are many painters who are capable of such a complex and lasting effect that their hold on the spirit is felt almost as a physical sensation. I never ceased to find this feeling in Bonnard; it seems soothing at first, even when it surprises; then it takes root, insidiously, its gentleness more tenacious than any amount o violence.

Bonnard holds up to the uninitiated eye a magic mirror in which everyday objects look as we think they are, and are nevertheless quite different from what they were before he showed them to us. Since that moment—and more so once the initial shock was past—Bonnard has been the point of reference to which I return in order to understand the extraordinary, and to accept the unacceptable.

JEAN CASSOU The best way to define the idea one has of an artist is to go back to one's first encounter with him and recall one's first youthful impressions. More reasoned judgements will come later, but one's subjective attitude will always be conditioned by that first impact. As for myself, I had no shock of discovery where Bonnard is concerned. I came to know and love his painting at an early age, but without any particular surprise, and at the same time as I was discovering and learning to love countless other things. But your first experience of Bonnard's painting was a crucial one; and I think we can take it as a point of departure. Let us start with what you say about his complexity.

RAYMOND COGNIAT I see that you agree that Bonnard's art is infinitely less simple than it seems at first. I find it hard to define it precisely, rather as Bonnard's forms and contours themselves are hard to define. For him this is a way of preserving their reality and mobility, not as objects but as pictorial elements. There is much more to Bonnard's art than this deliberate imprecision, which is not restricted to shapes alone. There are always several ways of looking at a picture or at an artist. Should we start by considering Bonnard the artist or Bonnard the man? Is it possible to distinguish between them? If so, what has this shy and retiring figure, glimpsed on the street, in common with the revolutionary genius of Bonnard the artist?

JEAN CASSOU I think you are right to emphasize the artistic viewpoint. Let us try to place him in the history of painting, with particular reference to the phenomenon which preceded him, Impressionism. It seems hard at first to define how he differs from it. At first sight he seems to offer us the same ingredients: representations of the external world—the air, the countryside, the sea—all in the same spirit of serene and joyous sensuality. Like Impressionism, Bonnard's art is realism. But there is a distinction to be made. I would make it like this: the Impressionists based their realism on a certain conception of reality. Of all the principles, the causes, the agents, that can be detected in reality they had chosen one: light. From light and its division into colours they deduced their whole system of painting, a coherent and logical system which excludes all other factors such as space, contour and form. Their universe is made of light and can be represented only through light: the universe becomes an opalescent pattern of colours, reflections, fleeting visions. For colours are fluid; they depend on the season, the weather, the hour, the minute, the second. One other factor is involved, one which is essential to this conception of the world, this 'physical theory': namely time. Bonnard is not involved in this conception of the world. He is in contact with natural realities: sky, plants, sunrise, sunset, spring, winter, the sea; but without seeking to express his reaction to the accidental 'modes' of these realities, without trying to depict their perpetual changes. It is the realities themselves that interest him, as they appear to him at the moment when he paints them and as he knows them to be, and enjoys them, at *any* moment. And as a painter he transforms these things into painting. The object is transfigured on the canvas, and not in the real world; not because of the position of the sun at the hour or season when the transfiguration takes place, but for artistic reasons, because certain touches of mauve set off certain touches of gold on the canvas.

Bonnard was always in close contact with nature, but he broke free of it in order to put on his canvas what we now call pure painting.

The Impressionists always stayed in contact with nature. Their eye, which is immensely subtle and curious, always eager for more and more delicate sensations, remains fixed on reality in order to catch its modifications, its transitions, and reproduce them as exactly as possible. Their art has been rightly described as absolutely non-intellectual and materialist.

Bonnard's eye is as acute as theirs. This is true not only when he is contemplating the spectacle of life but also—and more actively so—when he is placing paint on canvas and creating miraculous combinations of colour.

Much has been said, quite rightly, of the pantheism of the Impressionists. Their life, their very essence is bound up in the cosmos. The external world is their limit, and they cannot pass beyond it; this is their strength and their greatness. Bonnard is a ' pantheist ' too. He has always lived in and by nature. But he retains his independence; nature is not an absolute sov-

ereign to him. He plays with it, makes of it what he chooses; and the result is pure painting, capricious, arbitrary and often almost abstract. No effect of light, no climatic influence, none of the minute miracles which obsessed the Impressionists, can explain how a woman lying in her bath can become a streak of violet, nor how a dining-room wall, a bunch of flowers and a woman's face in the foreground can form one vast palpitation of faded roses, nor how a window can open and pour on to a summer lunch-table such a fantastic torrent of snowy splendour. Images like this spring from nature and a deep love of nature. But they are not nature, they are art.

RAYMOND COGNIAT   I think I agree with your definition of Bonnard's relationship with the Impressionists, and the way in which his treatment of nature differs from theirs. Nevertheless, it seems to me that he himself was an ultimate consequence of Impressionism, if not one that the works of Monet and Renoir would have allowed us to expect. He owes nothing to their use of colour; he often preferred the half-tones of interiors to the luminosity of the open air. But like them he wanted to paint the air, its vibration, its mobility in immobility and, in spite of what you say, its appearance at a certain moment in time. Like them he achieved subtle and revealing colour effects by juxtaposing tiny touches of colour. Like the Impressionists, he wanted to keep as close as possible to the reality of appearances; but in his reality there is something more, something hidden; he could not be content with external appearances.

You consider this idea of reality less important for him than his artistic individuality; this is because Bonnard appeared in the world of art at a time when all sorts of new ideas and experiments were in the air, when Symbolism was proclaiming a new mystical union between words and colours.

Seen in this historical context, Bonnard's painting reveals a subtle interplay of influences. The café scenes in the Boulevard de Clichy or the Place Blanche have something of Lautrec and even of Carrière, with unmistakable traces of *Modern' Style*. In his women at their toilet and his unexpected plunging perspectives there is something of Lautrec or Degas, with reminders of the foreshortening seen in photographs and in Japanese art. All this corroborates the emphasis you place on 'art' rather than 'nature.'

Bonnard's originality is still genuine, although time has altered our way of seeing. This art, which seems unadventurous to us today, is alive with new ideas and was intensely personal from the very beginning without provoking any such scandal as the *avant-garde* produced a few years later. Bonnard's art does not make its point by violence; it has none of the forcefulness of Cubism and Fauvism. It holds fast to its time and place. The cause of this restraint is not timidity but a great spiritual honesty. Gradually he learns

what he can do and what he wants to do; his thrifty palette grows richer year by year. His drawing has the same characteristics. It is not made up of improvised, arbitrary simplifications; it has no tendency to 'found a style'. Like his painting it is made up of little touches added to each other to create an atmosphere or a movement. He does not try to surprise by means of virtuosity but to suggest, as honestly as possible, the truth about his model—including, if possible, the model's feelings.

This peaceful, sure progress is the symbol of his whole existence.

One can seek and find a relationship between Bonnard's aesthetic and that of other artists, but the influence is never a profound one. Every theme, every technique that has caught his attention has been re-thought and seen anew by the artist himself. He invariably puts it to new purposes and thus makes it his own.

JEAN CASSOU Yes, he does. But if we were to leave it at that, we should see Bonnard only as a painter with astonishing resources of individual temperament and technique which he used to capture, with more devotion and more skill than the others, the line, colour and movement of the external world. If this were so, he would be no more than a wonderfully gifted *illustrator*. But this would be to neglect something absolutely fundamental about Bonnard's development: his growing freedom. Bonnard is in contact

13

with nature, I agree; but he is also one of those whose art leads one to think of painting as a phenomenon in its own right. All this done without an aesthetic theory, without an explicit intention, but modestly and calmly. He thought only of remaining true to nature; he was a sensitive artist, a very sensitive artist, and nothing more or less. That is how he saw himself (if he ever tried to define himself at all) and that is what he was. But this exceptional sensitivity became more exceptional still when applied to paint and canvas, when exercised in complete freedom in the creation of a work of pure painting. This is the miracle of Bonnard.

RAYMOND COGNIAT   I should like to go back to what I said a few moments ago about Bonnard's place in contemporary art. At various points in his career he impinged on the artistic history of the times without ever belonging to the major movements.

In the first place his temperament, and the setting in which he lived, made Bonnard from the very first an indispensable link between the art of the nineteenth and twentieth centuries, a link without which the transition would be abrupt and perhaps even inexplicable. Many works which seem cautious and restrained to us now were an adventurous gesture in his day. It is difficult today to understand how Puvis de Chavannes, Carrière and Albert Besnard could have been regarded as revolutionaries, how the artists of *La Revue Blanche*, recipients via Séru-

sier of the Breton gospel of Gauguin, could have represented the extreme of audacity. They sought no scandal, but were content to accept it. So there is no contradiction between Bonnard's shy and timid nature and the resolution with which he persisted in doing as he wished in spite of the public's lack of response.

The growing popular success of Impressionism had liberated the younger painters while at the same time making it vitally necessary for them to find their own personal style. Bonnard's first experiments carry the mark of certain contemporary trends, but it would be wrong to think of them as signs of indecision or hesitancy. At this moment, Bonnard—perhaps unconsciously, certainly unintentionally—held the balance between the opposing poles of Impressionism (now accepted) and what was to become Fauvism. This transitional role, which was not the result of prudence, was the role he continued to play all his life; he remained inseparably linked to his age, but never gave his allegiance to a doctrine. His rightful place, both chronologically and as an artist, is at the end of Impressionism and the beginning of modern art; but later, around 1920, his work was used to support the view that Cubism was not the only original way of viewing the world and reconstructing space; that the explosions of Fauvism were not the only way of renewing the artist's palette; that Expressionism did not exclude other ways of using the human face and form; that the nightmare visions of Surrealism

Two photographs taken by André Ostier in Bonnard's studio, 1941

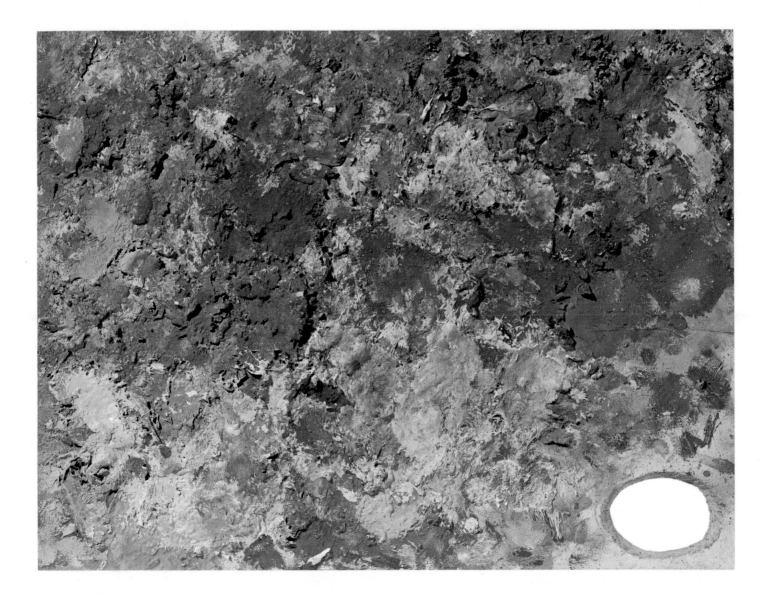

did not reveal all the secrets of the human mind. For the second time Bonnard provided proof that nature can be treated with great freedom without renouncing any of the sensitivity of the Impressionists, and without seeking to distort it systematically.

Later, after the last war, he showed, still without denying his past, how his art could be completely renewed without losing any of its freedom or its truthfulness. He knew how to create the sensation of space without using the distortions inherent in geometrical perspective and came close to the abstract without ever needing to use it, although his example served to justify its use by others. All this without ever repeating himself, without ever allowing himself to be imprisoned by a formula or by his own success.

The means Bonnard employed cannot be called formulas, although they are easy to catalogue precisely because they *are* means and not ends in themselves. His palette encompasses all the nuances of grey as well as the clash and the unexpected harmony of pink close to orange or mauve, so close indeed that the colours almost merge, gaining an astonishing intensity from the fact of juxtaposition. By these means Bonnard produces breathtaking effects where another would achieve nothing but confusion. Another of his characteristics is his love of painting against the light, of faces burning red even in shadow.

There is also his use of the unforeseen in composition, perspectives plunging into the distance, contrasts of proportion, combinations or juxtapositions of different planes. For instance a dining-table or wash-stand in the foreground occupies the greater part of the picture while the centre of interest lies much further back, perhaps even extended in depth by a mirror. And yet, in spite of its depth, the picture remains two-dimensional, so that no part of it is subordinated to another.

Above all, he had a highly personal conception of space, in which the object is never reduced to a flat surface, nor to a uniform colour, although the whole is a picture with its own unity of surface and density.

It is possible, as we have said, that it was originally photography that suggested to Bonnard his distortions, or rather his unorthodox proportions and his tricks of 'layout'. He drew from them unexpected and wholly personal effects, while ensuring that the picture on his easel remained a flat surface as a mural decoration always should. He never seems to have been very attracted by mural painting as such, or perhaps he was not asked often enough to do it. The few samples he gave us are of remarkable quality and very interesting in themselves, but they contribute nothing new to their genre nor to the painter's own technical development. Perhaps an artist as independent as Bonnard would have found it hard to adapt himself to the discipline imposed by the size and shape of the surface available.

JEAN CASSOU   No, he would not have been able to adapt himself to the discipline of the wall in architecture, just as he never submitted to the discipline of the picture-frame.   And yet we agree that his art is two-dimensional. He reduces the external world, or rather 'what he paints', to a single plane; this does not mean that he shuts it up inside a frame; that is something intellectual artists try to do, artists whose pictures are structured objects in themselves. He is not a structural artist; his vision overflows the frame. But it takes shape on a plane surface.

And this is where I think he parts company with the sensualism and the materialism of the Impressionists, the many-coloured profusion of their images, and comes close to our present-day view of painting.

RAYMOND COGNIAT   I agree.   The key to his system is revealed by the mirror he so often uses in his pictures.   A mirror placed on a wall adds a space and depth which break up the unity of the flat surface. This glimpse of another dimension is sharply delineated by a rectangle which cuts arbitrarily across the lines of the composition. This sudden distension in the middle of a flat wall is the same as that produced by an open window, but the window opens on to a distant, generally unbounded prospect, or at any rate on to an extension of the space within the room.

A window is an escape from the tangible immediate surroundings; a mirror turns the eye back on itself. It traps us between what is in front and what is behind.   Even when he does not introduce a mirror, Bonnard always succeeds in creating this feeling of silent isolation.   This defines the difference between Bonnard and the Impressionists very exactly: if you look at Renoir's *Les Grands Boulevards*, Pissarro's *L'Avenue de l'Opéra*, Monet's *Les Jardins du Louvre*, the impression is always that of an open window. The painter stands in front of his subject and outside it.   Now look at Bonnard's Montmartre street-scenes (*Le Boulevard de Clichy, La Place Blanche*, etc.); the painter is inside his subject. He sits beside or among the watchers at the café tables who obscure a large part of the view. Even in street-scenes, then, Bonnard encloses us in the immediate situation, makes us rub shoulders with reality; even without a mirror he encloses us in an intimate world.

JEAN CASSOU   Bonnard is never outside but inside his subject, and this is what brings him close to the ultimate consequences of present-day painting. Having abandoned all representation, however distorted, it has no view of reality. It does not contemplate reality from any point of view whatever. I have just been calling to mind some of Bonnard's most magnificent paintings, and reflecting that he is not an external observer of reality any more than abstract artists are. He is in the middle of it. Reality for him is not a 'spectacle', but a source of art, a stimulus, a

19

motive force for art. It is not for him to take up his position in front of it and contemplate it in order to reproduce it. His place is inside it, so that the dimensions and relative positions of the objects are overthrown, their relationships disappear, there is neither up nor down, length nor breadth; a thousand details of colour dominate the total effect. The product of this situation will not be a picture of the scene; it will be painting in its own right, autonomous and absolute.

And yet Bonnard never forgets what it is that has involved him in this situation : reality. Even in some of the extremely stylized masterpieces of his last period it is impossible not to be aware that the source of all his art is a profound feeling for nature. Think of Bonnard the man and his response to nature : his miraculous sensory apparatus in a perpetual state of excitation, savouring shadows, lights and scents. My last memory of him dates from shortly before he died. Spring was already in the air in the little garden at Le Cannet as I walked with the old man and saw him gently finger the first buds of the year. You know that his last painting, to which he was putting the final touches in the days before he died, is a mimosa in bloom. He lived in hope of spring until the very end of his life.

RAYMOND COGNIAT After one has tried to analyse all the essential qualities of his art, at once so simple and so complex, I think that the true secret, the essential Bonnard, lies in what you have just said. But I should like now to isolate one aspect of his complexity.

In spite of his modesty, his individualism, his love of nature, Bonnard's art seems to me to possess social as well as an artistic significance. It embodies a whole society and a whole age. Even his discretion is a characteristic of the society rather than the painter : it is the reflection of a cultivated bourgeois society, secure in its refinement and its hatred of excess.

Bonnard's favourite subjects belong to the intimate, even the secret, life of this society. Women in their dressing-rooms, modest in their nudity, their poses lacking any trace of provocativeness; families coming together for tea in the garden; the daily intimacy of meal-times. Bonnard never paints the parts of the house where people work or receive visitors. That belongs to public rather than private life. He belongs to a world where leisure is an important part of existence.

This society was essentially inward-looking, and in its well-upholstered apartments it stood aloof from social change. Bonnard's painting blends into this setting. It reflects the hangings, the silent carpets, the curtains which filter the light of day. The colours are not brutal but the greys are never completely grey. The harmony between Bonnard and his social setting is so natural and clear that when, later, his style became more astringent, his colours more intense, his contrasts less discreet, this happened at the precise moment when his class was awakening, coming out of its shell, letting fresh air into its houses and into its mind, tearing down the ornate wallpapers and hangings, painting its walls plain white. Bonnard's boldness is never a revolt, never fundamentally out of sympathy with contemporary developments.

JEAN CASSOU   This bourgeois world, which received not only Bonnard but also his friend Vuillard and all the group of the Nabis, was a world of cultivated *nouveaux riches*, industrialists with their minds open to new social ideas, such as Arthur Fontaine, the Natansons, the people Vuillard painted and who hung his paintings on their walls. It was largely this society that defeated the forces of reaction in the Dreyfus affair and solidly established the Third Republic. This victory did not come without a struggle. At the turn of the century the air was full of unrest and of threats of war. But the status quo was to last for a long time yet, and these last years of the nineteenth century, and the first years of the twentieth, give an impression above all of vitality and self-assurance. It is not surprising that the art of the period carries the same stamp.

RAYMOND COGNIAT   There is no revolutionary fervour in Bonnard, even when he is at his most original. However extreme the position he adopts, Bonnard is never a destroyer. What he gives us is always a harmonious solution.

JEAN CASSOU   A harmonious solution... Yes, I agree; even when he is enjoying a joke, when he is ironic or impertinent or sharp, when he adds a dash of pepper or the Attic salt of *La Revue Blanche*, there is no discordance, no bitterness. His art is basically happy. He is inviting us to a restoration of the rule of Nature; and in that golden age there can be neither ill-will nor defiance.

RAYMOND COGNIAT   Does Bonnard's art tell us anything about the future? As things are at the moment, he seems to represent an end rather than a beginning. The succeeding generation gives evidence of a need for forcefulness, explosiveness even, which is quite alien to him. Most present day experiments constitute, in one way or another, a denial of everything that painting has been up to now, both in choice of medium and in choice of technique and subject.

Bonnard's art remains linked to the past. Our conversation has illustrated this; we have constantly been led to consider it in relation to what came before it, namely Impressionism. Bonnard makes no clean break, although his example shows that there is always something new to be said with materials that have been used before. He seeks no new techniques, affects no ignorance of what his predecessors have done. He could not be called backward-looking, but he is the product of his past; and he will find a place in the galleries alongside traditional works more easily than, say, Picasso, or Kandinsky, or even Fernand Léger. By its nature, his sensibility

21

appeals to individual meditation rather than collective enthusiasm.

Bonnard's art is not for the masses. It is not an art that can adapt itself to a mechanical world. Nor is it suitable for places full of noise and movement. It is nevertheless possible that even this world will contain a few spirits who will accept Bonnard as a sort of compensation, a welcome antithesis of the goal towards which we seem to be travelling. He provides repose and release from tension in this way, but there is infinitely more to him than that.

He is the final product of a whole society, a whole conception of man, perhaps a whole civilization, which is approaching its end. Thanks to him this end is not a humiliation but a final flowering which there will still be some to appreciate and remember with affection.

JEAN CASSOU There is no alternative but to accept historical change, however revolutionary. This means that a new image of the universe must be accepted too, and thus a new art, quite distinct from everything that art has been from the days of the cave-painters until now. But must we also give up our love of gardens?

I accept that we are living through one of those moments in history when even the things we still possess seem virtually to belong to the past. On the other side of the abyss is the unknown future towards which we must launch ourselves, not in a *salto mortale* but in a *salto vitale*. In that new world, art will have changed completely. It will have nothing in common with the culture which I still call ours because we have inherited it; that culture will belong to the past. So be it. There is even something attractive about this moment of decision—like a monologue in *Hamlet*. And yet, is nothing to be saved from the wreck? Will the man of to-morrow be completely new? He will create other arts. He has already created works which fit into none of the accepted categories such as painting or sculpture. And yet I think that some things will live on, or perhaps I should say live again. I was half-dreaming when I spoke to you of the love of gardens, but a conversation like ours, disjointed as it may be, leaves gaps in which dreams may come to the surface. This love of gardens, is it not independent of the great upheavals of history? As he senses the coming of spring in the tender buds of a frail tree, Bonnard is oblivious of the revolutions of history and is aware only of a revolution of a different order, one which escapes our chronologies by repeating itself every year.

The mystery of simplicity is perhaps the most unfathomable of all mysteries. However critical the situations we envisage, however cataclysmic their consequences, however cruel our dilemmas, however painful our resolve to start again with a clean slate, a certain humble reality will continue to flower. This simplicity is not a return to the past, but an absolute: unexpected, unexplained, without links with past or future —in other words, something very like a miracle. This is why I have been talking about the mystery of simplicity. This is a mystery which needs no fathoming. There is no need to ask why a Corot landscape, a La Fontaine fable, a Bonnard, exists. That question would limit us to the temporal world of cause and effect. In discussing Bonnard, we have been obliged, as critics and historians, to try to situate him in relation to time : his time, our time, even the times to come. But having done that, it was our duty to allot to him his true place, which is outside time. Whatever the future may have in store for us, the miracle of simplicity will always be possible; and it will come at the moment when it is least expected.

Eragny, 1894.   Photograph : Edouard Vuillard

Roussel, Vallotton, Luce, Ranson, Sérusier and Bonnard, c.1900.
Photograph : Edouard Vuillard

Roussel and his children, Lucy Hessel and Pierre Bonnard, c.1909.
Photograph : Edouard Vuillard

Bonnard's Ford, 8023 E 4, at L'Etang-la-Ville in 1923.
Photograph : Jacques Salomon

Roussel, his daughter Annette, Bonnard, Claude Anet and Marthe
Bonnard at La Jacannette in 1921. Photograph : Jacques Salomon

Bonnard and Roussel, c.1930.   Round spectacles have replaced
the pince-nez.   Photograph : Edouard Vuillard

Pierre Bonnard, photographed by Alfred Natanson (Alfred Athis), c.1892

Lithograph for Petites Scènes familières

THE JOY OF SEEING

I found the photograph in a box with a lot of others. It fascinates me. There are no shadows, and the almost invisible summer landscape gives a strange intensity to the gaze of the figure.

At that time my father was starting to use his big Nadar-style camera to photograph the young artists of *La Revue Blanche* who came to stay with my uncle Thadée and his wife Misia, first at Valvins and later at their house Le Relais at Villeneuve-sur-Yonne.

His huge lips exaggerated by the camera, Lautrec sleeps in a deckchair in the garden. Vuillard, Roussel, Vallotton and Romain Coolus stand with their hands on each other's shoulders, smiling, with their youthful beards framing un-

lined faces. The future lies before them like a summer day.

Bonnard is different. He is twenty-five and looks twenty. Photographed alone, his crooked cravat emerging from a heavy reefer-jacket, he still looks the same short-sighted schoolboy who used to bring prize-books home to his grandmother. A wayward moustache and a few wisps of hair under his lower lip give a sort of timid virility to his innocent features. His great startled brown eyes almost seem pressed against the steel-rimmed pince-nez for fear of missing anything of the world which lies before him, the world he will soon transfigure. His work resembles no-one else's, and Bonnard was like

27

Woman in Petticoat,
lithograph for L'Escarmouche

FOUR PANELS FOR A SCREEN, 1892-1898
WOMAN IN WHITE-SPOTTED DRESS
SEATED WOMAN WITH CAT
WOMAN IN CHECK DRESS
WOMAN IN BLUE CAPE

28

29

no-one else. He was thin; it seemed that he was deliberately so, as if from modesty. He was shy to the point of eccentricity, and he reacted strongly against any threat of a display of emotion, even from those closest to him. He was taciturn and sometimes caustic in his manner, but just because he said little he had the gift of expressing what he really wanted to express, however simple or however profound.

It seems difficult to tell the story of his life in such a way that it will have a beginning, a middle and an end; there are no Pink or Blue Periods, and words seem strangely irrelevant. It is his painting—the colours woven in wild harmonies like some astonishing silken material seen from the wrong side—that liberates the essence of his life and sets it before us. Bonnard was a revolutionary in art but he had been born a bourgeois, and he led a bourgeois-bohemian existance from year to year, from season to season, moving from sparsely furnished flat to bare studio, and on to a room in some hotel.

He himself, with tin tubes pressed against a board, has told the story of his life, filling our eyes with the miracles of everyday life which without him we should never be able to see.

Since Bonnard made so little use of language in communicating with us, I shall venture to describe my own first contact with him at the age of two. My first impressions came from a little painting by Bonnard which hung above my father's writing-desk: a young woman sitting on her bed to put on her black stockings. To me it represented my grandfather. The curls

on the model's cheek must have looked to a small child like the beard of my poor maternal grandfather, ironically named Fortuné Mellot. When my mother took me to see him in his little grey bungalow at Boulogne-sur-Seine, we always found him sitting with his back rounded like the girl in the picture.

Visual analogies are curious things. Just as a cloud fleetingly takes the shape of a profile, Bonnard's malicious line often contains an ambiguity. Collectors who are in the habit of gazing at their favourite pictures every day often suddenly come across the answer to the riddle: a cow looking over a hedge, a white bull, or part of a figure, lost in the shadow.

Illustration for Marie

Lithograph for Petites Scènes familières

EYES THAT OPEN

Our journey begins at Fontenay-aux-Roses, a place which, a hundred years ago, still deserved its fragrant name. There, on 3 October, 1867, Pierre Bonnard was born of a father from Dauphiné, Eugène Bonnard, a senior official at the War Ministry, and an Alsatian mother, Elise Mertzdorff.

His brother Charles, who was to be a chemist and work in the vineyards of Algeria, was the eldest child. Later there was to be a sister, Andrée, a born musician.

Boarding-school, gilt buttons on his uniform, the high-school at Vanves, then the Lycée Louis le Grand and the Lycée Charlemagne : Pierre worked hard. He loved literature and the dead languages and later came to love philosophy.

But most of all he loved the freedom of the holidays in Dauphiné, at Le Grand-Lemps, a large village at the foot of the Terres-Froides, facing the mountains of the Isère. At his family's house, Le Clos, the garden merged into an orchard. A farm adjoined the house. There was the monumental figure of his grandmother Mme Mertzdorff tucking up her white apron to feed grain to the chickens. There were geese, rabbits, goats; it was here that Pierre discovered his affinity with animals, all animals. All his life he was to feel more in common with them than with most human beings.

M. Bonnard, with his beard and his smoking-cap, was a stern figure, devoted equally to his

31

The Artist's Father, brush drawing

He had chosen two equally ambitious subjects : *Hierarchy in the Civil Service*, on which he failed the oral examination, and *The Triumph of Mardochee*, a bravura piece, now lost, a 'great big oriental sort of thing' which the judges refused to take seriously.

Pierre went to work under one of his father's friends, a lawyer in the public prosecutor's office. This man was an easy-going employer, and dust gathered on the briefs while Pierre filled with incisive little pen drawings *La Vie du Peintre*, his record of his day-to-day life.

In the year of grace 1889 we find him living with his grandmother in the Rue de Parme and renting his first studio in the Batignolles district, in the Rue Le Chapelais. At this moment the hand of Providence intervened to remove the remaining obstacles between him and his chosen career. *France-Champagne* paid him a hundred francs for a poster design he had timidly submitted. At this news Bonnard *père*, at Le Clos, threw his smoking-cap over the moon and decided to allow his son to become a painter.

Another historic moment had been the meeting at the Pension Gloanec at Pont-Aven in September 1888 between Sérusier and Gauguin.

At the Bois · d'Amour Sérusier had been touched by grace and had painted on the lid of a cigar-box, at Gauguin's dictation, a landscape of pure colours synthesized into strange shapes, which he called *Le Talisman*, and which he brought back to Paris in October of the same year. In a half-mystical, half-farcical spirit, he gave the name of 'Nabis' (a Hebrew word meaning prophet, suggested to him by his friend

library and to his orchard of cherry and pear trees and the essences he cultivated. But when the holidays were over, and when Pierre had passed his *baccalauréat*, decisions had to be taken. The choice lay between two equally gloomy prospects : the civil service and the Bar.

Bored with his legal studies, Pierre started to attend classes at the Ecole des Beaux-Arts. He also worked at the Académie Julian in the Faubourg Saint-Denis, where the twenty-five-year-old *massier* or treasurer of the studio, Paul Sérusier, was the first to give him encouragement. There he made friends with Maurice Denis, Ibels, Paul Ranson and Félix Vallotton. In spite of all this he got his degree at the age of twenty. But he was to fail, almost simultaneously, the civil service competition and the *Prix de Rome*.

32

YOUNG WOMAN AT A WINDOW, 1898

Cazalis) to the young friends—Ibels, Bonnard, Ranson, Maurice Denis and later Vuillard and Roussel—who were initiated into his new fellowship. 'Thus,' says Denis, 'we learned that every work of art is a transposition, a distortion, the passionate equivalent of some sensory experience.'

Later, Vollard, who was not one to be unduly concerned about nuances, gave his version of the whole episode. According to this, Sérusier announced on his return to Julian's studio in the autumn: 'I have met a genius. His name is Gauguin, and he has revealed to me the true secret of painting: "If you want to paint an apple, paint a circle!"'

The doctrine exemplified by the magic cigar-box was rather less laconic than this. Gauguin's intention was to turn the younger generation towards 'a whole plastic conception of the universe.'

At Sérusier's side stood another tireless proselyte, the eighteen-year-old Maurice Denis, who was learned far beyond his years. Verkade describes him as being 'like a young girl who had never left her mother.'

'Gauguin was the master,' Denis was to write later. 'The secret of his hold on us was that he furnished one or two very simple but inescapable truths at a time when we had no information to guide us.' With his long fair locks, his biblical countenance illumined by the ardour of a neophyte (and by his copious libations), Sérusier—'Nabi of the Shining Beard'—had the look of an apostle posing for a Bock advertisement.

His father, a director of the Houbigant perfume company, had intended him to go into business. He had had a brilliant academic career. He knew the philosophy and the art of all the ages, and he was a forceful and subtle orator. Arms spread wide to receive his converts, he never ceased to preach, with a touching sincerity, the gospel revealed to him in Brittany.

Once a month the Nabis dined together at the Os à Moelle in the Passage Brady. This *bistro* had acquired its name of 'The Marrow Bone' from the large bone the proprietor had attached to the key of the 'smallest room'.

During and after the meal, the prophets expounded their theories. But although Sérusier's dogmatism offered an antidote to Naturalist ideas, Bonnard was reluctant, as was Vuillard, to submit to any system which claimed to solve all artistic problems at one blow. But he was happy in the company of the enthusiasts, let them talk, watched from behind his pince-nez with his amused air of perpetual surprise, and when he spoke it was usually to answer some question by saying 'I disagree entirely'. He hated taking part in theoretical discussions. Jan Verkade, a close friend, whose great height led Sérusier to christen him *Le Nabi obéliscal*, says of Bonnard, 'He had the ability to conceal his genius beneath an almost frivolous attitude. Like Vuillard, he believed in intuition.'

But although his contact with Gauguin's Symbolism strengthened his natural indepen-

BOATING AT CHATOU, 1896

dence of spirit, it left him with new perspectives and the habit of reflection.

Holidays give one's ideas space to breathe... it must have been beautiful at Le Grand-Lemps in the summer of 1889. His grandmother had written to him: 'My dear Pierre... At the moment I am shelling young peas in the dining-room with the dog lying at my feet and the two cats under the table. I hear a snuffling noise and the cow's head appears at the window. Outside the little maid is shouting "Joseph, the calf's loose!..."'

Pierre drank in the beauty of the landscapes that had (did he know?) delighted Jongkind. He remembered Corot's advice: 'Never lose sight of the first impression.' It might have been spoken with Bonnard in mind. All his work, although it always matured in his memory, never betrays its origin in the little sketches in which

away by painting the *Mother and Child*. This was rather an unhappy experiment, but there is a *graffito* full of humour which shows Bonnard himself as a footslogger in the Military Training-

The Military Training-Ground, pen drawing

he captured moments of life in all their freshness and immediacy.

The partridges, the bedroom, the castle he had so conscientiously painted the year before now seemed too limiting. He tried to break

Ground and which looks forward to the joyous *L'Exercice*, with its red képis and trousers and its reminiscences of Gauguin and 'Nabism'.

In 1890 Bonnard, Vuillard and Denis shared a pocket-handkerchief-sized studio in the Rue

Pigalle. When Lugné-Poë joined them, fresh from his military service, he often had no money to contribute towards the rent, so he tried to sell his friends' pictures for a hundred or two hundred francs each to theatrical people. One night he succeeded in selling a Vuillard water-colour to Coquelin the younger for his dressing-room wall.

Back in the Rue Pigalle, Lugné brought along Antoine, a former Gas Board employee who had decided to live by his dream, the 'Free Theatre'. A dealer appeared to take a look at the canvases in the studio: his name was Le Barc de Boutteville.

Bonnard and Vuillard worked side by side, went about together, visited art galleries. And at the Goupil gallery, where they went to see the Van Goghs, they liked the Renoirs, Degas, Monets that Sérusier had no time for. At the Galerie Tanguy they discovered Cézanne.

A sudden revelation : the exhibition of Japanese art at the Ecole des Beaux-Arts. The Hiro-shighe prints which delighted them were, for a time, to come between them and their habitual subjects. Bonnard's Parisiennes take on a sur-prising aspect at this period; as they clutch their hats in the wind, or lift their skirts to cross the street, they imitate the stilted grace of the geisha. And Vuillard, seduced by the harmonies of asymmetry, twists and contorts his seamstresses and housewives.

The fact that they worked together and shared common enthusiasms necessarily gave a passing resemblance to the experiments on which the two friends were engaged.

Parisiennes, lithograph for La Revue Blanche, *1895*

Bonnard, *le Nabi japonard*, was so bewitched by the charm of the pseudo-oriental that he pinned up on his wall nineteen-sou prints from the 'China and Japan' counter of the Grands Magasins du Printemps. At Le Clos, his sister, walking her dogs between one Bach fugue and the next, her nose pink from the fresh air, became *Woman with Rabbit*, drawn in a spiral, *Young Lady with Cat, Young Girl Shaking a Tablecloth*—the stylized heroine of tiny decorative pictures. Seeing her play croquet with her friends, Pierre cuts out their check dresses and flattens the pattern without a fold against the background of greenery.

During an idyllic August Charles Bonnard, a sergeant-dispenser at Grenoble, came over on Saturdays with an army friend, Claude Terrasse. This jovial giant, booming and bushy-haired, taught music at a Dominican school at Arcachon in civilian life. The future composer of *Les Travaux d'Hercule* and *La Fiancée du Scaphandrier* lost his heart to the grave charm of Andrée Bonnard. She was seventeen years old. They were married that autumn.

In addition to the dinners at L'Os à Moelle, the Nabis used to meet every Saturday afternoon in the studio of Paul Ranson at 25, Boulevard du Montparnasse; this was known as the 'Temple'. France Ranson, a young woman of great vitality, who bore the title of Light of the Temple, gave them beer and sandwiches and sometimes rum punch. Sérusier painted their host in Nabical costume, holding the crozier which was passed to each speaker in the course of their meetings.

Paul Ranson came from the Limoges area. Naturally ebullient despite his Calvinist origins, he painted pictures and tapestry-cartoons inspired at one and the same time by medieval art, theosophy and *Modern' Style*. Gauguin visited the 'Temple' three or four times. He was an odd sort of messiah with his Breton waistcoat and his hoarse, mocking, Parisian voice; he had left his carved wooden clogs behind somewhere along the way. Talking inexhaustibly, emptying glasses of punch, he was a different man from the melancholy conqueror who was to confess his poverty when he returned from the fortunate isles. Did Bonnard know that Lautrec called Gauguin a 'pompous pundit'? The Nabis had clubbed together to buy a Gauguin picture which each man kept for a week at a time. Bonnard often had to be reminded when his turn came round.

The 'Temple' was not only a place for discussion; there was entertainment too. Ranson had built a marionette theatre whose principal character, the Abbé Prout,—an unctuous cleric who continually rubbed his hands exclaiming 'Good! Good! Good!'—was later to transfer to the Salon of the same Mme Strauss-Bizet who was to suggest more than one trait of Proust's Oriane.

Poster for La Revue Blanche, lithograph, 1894

40   *In the Street, wash drawing*

PARIS OMNIBUS

Bonnard's Paris, *fin de siècle*. The Paris of thin fiacre-horses and mighty omnibus-horses. Horse-buses whose conductors stopped the percherons by pulling the end of a string attached to the leg of the driver. At the bottom of the Rue des Martyrs stood a row of placid relief-horses. Autumn rains, old-time winter snows, April hail, from which the red-faced bus-driver was protected by his wide-brimmed hat of *papier mâché*. The fiacre-drivers in white top-hats and beige frock-coats. Pedestrians crossing the street in all directions. Little men harnessed to handcarts. The din of iron-tyred wheels. Gloomy black *voitures à galerie*, followed by paupers who offered to lift trunks for forty sous.

Gleaming carriages on streets paved with wood-blocks or cobble-stones.

> *Tired with waiting in the lane*
> *I threw three stones and broke the pane*
> *But you still would not appear...*

When the wooden blocks became old and loose they went to feed the smoky fires of the furtive poor. It was the period when the bourgeoisie used to warm themselves by great stoves like the Choubersky (which killed Zola) and the potbellied Salamandre with its mica windows that glowed red with heat. Oil-lamps were fed by Saxoléine, the product advertised by Chéret in his tenderest pastel shades.

La Place Clichy, pen drawing

Bonnard's Parisian territory extended (apart from a short exile in Auteuil just after the Great War) from Batignolles to Montmartre. In the Place Clichy he could be seen advancing resolutely, bowler-hatted, on the still-safe carriageway, with Vuillard in an opera-hat and Ker Roussel in an artist's felt hat and an Inverness cape. At the foot of the statue of Marshal Moncey, apparently taking crooked flight in the middle of the square, the little flower-girl held out her bunches of violets.

In front of the Moulin Rouge, in the Place Blanche, Lautrec passes, flanked by his interminable cousin and scapegoat, Gabriel Tapié de Celeyran, *Tapir le Scélérat*. In the opposite direction, the *Nabi aux belles icônes*, Maurice Denis, hurries as fast as his plump legs will carry him, a manuscript under his arm, bearing some important piece of news.

Clichy-Odéon. A cuirassier sits on the top of the Panthéon to Courcelles horse-bus, celebrated in song by Georges Courteline, set to music by Claude Terrasse and lithographed by Bonnard. An orderly rank of cabs forms a frieze. Plump nursemaids, seen from behind, with crimped ribbons in their bonnets. An elegant lady bends over a beplumed infant learning to walk. Two urchins with a rather Japanese air play with a hoop. A stringy dog shakes itself. Bonnard must have enjoyed assembling these grotesques, against the empty background of an imaginary garden, on four leaves of a folding screen.

Cats stretch themselves to the full height of the picture, arching their backs hugely. Dogs

THE FRUIT-SELLER, 1899

43

frolic in every field and in the road, mongrels born only to disport themselves in unidentifiable wastelands. The characteristic distortions, the malicious gaucherie of his line, remind me of shy Bonnard stepping one day on my mother's delicate foot and offering her a madrigal by way of apology : 'A butterfly upon a rose...'

Mother still laughed at this memory many years later, just as we still smiled with pleasure at Bonnard's alert silhouettes.

Poster-columns, newspaper kiosks, urinals. Areas of wall set aside for the advertising, in large letters, of big respectable shops. Between the *Enseigne de Gersaint* and Lautrec's *confetti* could be seen Daumier's sack of coal for the *Entrepôt d'Ivry*, all of them doomed to peel and hang in tatters on the walls.

In 1891 Bonnard set off, his head in the clouds, to look for the *France-Champagne* poster which had just been published. Lautrec, for his part, was very struck by the poster. He went around for some time asking people 'Do you know Bonnard?' He was not content until Bonnard had taken him to the studio of Ancourt, the printer, where *Le Père Cotelle* officiated, caressing the lithographic stones with the crown of his greasy old cap. Bonnard's bare-shouldered, laughing girl, rising from the sparkling foam, showed Lautrec the way he was to travel as a poster artist, and she marks the beginning of an all-too-short friendship. In Bonnard, Lautrec could discern the immense promise of a talent which was about to come to flower. In the studio in the Rue Pigalle, he found Vuillard's little

cartoons. Full of enthusiasm, he set off in a carriage to take a few of their works on what proved to be a depressing round of the dealers. His new friends were delighted by his kindness. He tried to make them drink—he was obsessed by it—but he only succeeded once, at the memorable party he organized at the house of Alexandre Natanson in the Rue du Bois in 1895. There, dressed as a barman in a white coat, his head shaven, he took a temporary vow of silence and plied the assembled intelligentsia with fearsome cocktails. When Bonnard and Vuillard arrived late, hungry and thirsty after a healthy country walk, they were easy game. By dawn they lay dead to the world in a bedroom also occupied by the snoring Fénéon.

The first issue of *La Revue Blanche* had appeared on 1 October, 1891. Twenty years later the name heard in adult conversations was to sound to our childish ears like that of a once-beloved, dead princess : *La Revue Blanche... La Revue Blanche...* We asked no questions. Later we learned that the offices of this periodical in the Rue Laffitte (and previously in the Rue des Martyrs) had seen the beginning of some indestructible friendships : Tristan Bernard and Franc-Nohain, Félix Fénéon, Romain Coolus, Léon Blum, and all the painters who were still regular visitors to our house. We did not know that they had once called themselves Nabis. Nabism is a protected trademark today and a useful term for art-historians, but the artists themselves had left its adolescent mock-solemnity behind when they left the attic studios of their youth. Their names

The Dogs, lithograph for L'Escarmouche, 1893.

remained inseparably linked : Bonnard, Vuillard, Vallotton, Maurice Denis, Paul Sérusier.

Lugné-Poë opened his Maison de l'Oeuvre with a production of *Pelléas et Mélisande* in a prosaic theatre called the Bouffes du Nord. There, on the floor of the wardrobe store, the young painters painted on top of the faded Louis XV scenery new sets free from *trompe-l'œil* effects, a décor fit for the glacial drama of the Scandinavians. It was not all austerity, however; Bonnard worked on *La Dernière Croisade*, and Maurice Denis lithographed the programme for Tristan Bernard's *Les Pieds nickelés*. Turning the pages of fourteen years' issues of *La Revue Blanche*, I catch sight of my mother : between two pages, a badly-printed photograph is fading like ghosts at break of day. Unretouched, in her Symbolist costume, this young girl fresh from the provinces and the conservatoire is the *Antonia* of Dujardin or the heroine of *Rosmersholm*. At the Maison de l'Oeuvre she met Bonnard and Vuillard, who designed her costumes, as well as the whole *Revue Blanche* group. We can easily forget how young the contributors to *La Revue Blanche* sometimes were. My father, admittedly the youngest of the group, was sixteen when he contributed his first reviews and his first (and last) poems.

In that last decade of the nineteenth century, the intellectuals, like everyone else, had a robust sense of humour. Ibsenian caricatures from the 'Punch and Judy for Grown-up Children' like *Le recteur Krott* and the crone Bik were forerunners of Ubu without sharing his thunderous

gusto. When *Ubu Roi*, with its explosive '*Merdre*', had its dress-rehearsal at the Maison de L'Œuvre, Fernand Gregh (still a long way from his Academician's cocked hat) rose to answer Ubu's repeated cries of 'Shitrre' with his own 'Eatrre' ('*Mange-re*').

'My dear Charles,' wrote Pierre to his brother, 'since Grandmother left Paris I have found a lodging near the Place Clichy where I hope you will visit me next year. The view over an outer boulevard is very amusing...'

65, Rue de Douai. From his window, Pierre can see the roofs and chimneys, the bird-cage in the corner of an attic window. Along the boulevard there are benches, and thin trees that struggle through holes in the pavement, imprisoned in their heavy, cast-iron grilles. In summer the shops lower their striped blinds. A woman in a woollen shawl stops by the barrow of the fruit-seller. The goatherd passes by in his

Right : cover of Album de la Revue Blanche, lithograph, 1895

ALBUM DE LA REVUE BLANCHE

smock. A feminine shadow breaks away to join
the sun. There is a fiacre-horse with heavy blin-
kers. In winter the children set off for school in
their big hoods like unruly miniature monks. A
procession of young girls in surprising hats. On
the empty roadway, a little laundress staggers
along with a heavy basket and an umbrella too
big for her. And always a dog or several dogs,
hanging about. Pierre watches, draws, paints.

Alongside these intimate street scenes he places
little scenes of domestic life. Plump-cheeked
babies, children with napkins round their necks;
and on the staves of his brother-in-law's *Petit
Solfège Illustré* his minims become fat ladies, not
so solid as the crotchets, and a triplet becomes
three young ladies in mourning under the same
umbrella.

Claude Terrasse was more like a jack-in-the-
box than anything else. No-one would have
been surprised to find goat-legs and a cloven
hoof under his rumpled, corkscrew trousers, and
the only reason why he didn't play the pan-pipes
was that someone had taught him the piano.
His red thatch was a mass of curls. His beard
revealed an extraordinarily red mouth, avid for
all sorts of pleasures, and behind his pince-nez
twinkled two endearing forget-me-not blue
eyes. Since his marriage to Andrée Bonnard he
had left the Dominicans of Arcachon for the
little organ of the church of La Trinité, and it
was in his studio in the Rue Ballu that the
Théâtre des Pantins performed. What has happened I wonder, to the scripts of the ephemeral
works they put on? There were other produc-

Sketch for a screen

48

THE TERRASSE CHILDREN WITH THE DOG BLACK, 1902

Cover of Le Petit Solfège Illustré, 1893

tions besides a revival of *Ubu Roi* and the first performance of *Vive la France !*, an obscene operetta by Franc-Nohain that was soon banned by the censorship. Terrasse played the piano; Franc-Nohain and Jarry—dressed in cycling gear and very particular about the intricacies of the rhythm—worked the marionettes, of which

there were many, all made and painted on his big table by Bonnard. In front of the stage were fifty seats, all of them very dear : something like five francs. The performance, which was eccentric and uninhibited, lasted no more than an hour. The occasional bourgeois who appeared, duped by the dithyrambs of a few friendly

WOMAN IN BLUE HAT, 1908

The Umbrellas, pen drawing

journalists, used to lose their tempers and shout that it was all a fraud. One night a gentleman refused to leave and banged on the curtain with his cane.

This courageous enterprise, a good half-century ahead of its time, soon came to an end. Fortunately, Bonnard had lithographed covers for ten or so of the most successful songs in the repertoire, in particular Franc-Nohain's punning *Chansons de la Charcutière*: *La Malheureuse Adèle* (*'Elle est morte, Adèle'*) *'Ris, Yette de Tours'* from *Le Pays Tourangeau*, and *Velas ou l'Officier de fortune* (*'Sers, Velas, sers ta patrie'*) a patriotic song.

In 1891 Bonnard had sent nine pictures to the Salon des Indépendants, and had a group exhibition with the other Nabis at Le Barc de Boutteville's gallery. There, in 1892, his work attracted the attention of Roger Marx and Albert Aurier. Gustave Geffroy referred to its 'violent tachism'. Bonnard's colours, still clear at this time, were to become subdued for a while. In 1894 the *Revue Blanche* poster was to adorn the walls of Paris with its fragrant shades of grey.

Vollard, to whose tiny shop in the Rue Laffitte Bonnard had been taken by Denis, published Bonnard's album of lithographs, *Quelques Aspects de la Vie de Paris* ('Some Aspects of Paris Life') with its arresting little figures. In it Helleu recognized his wife and daughter walking in the *Avenue du Bois de Boulogne*. In 1895 Bonnard adorned the cover of the album of Nabi prints from *La Revue Blanche* with a long young woman in black, carrying a whip and playing with her white dog. On one page of the album one of

MISIA GODEBSKA, 1908-1909

Woman with Umbrella, lithograph

Bonnard's Parisiennes, in black enlivened by a touch of red, climbs the stairs. Lautrec, always eager for novelty, decided at the beginning of the year to insert into the review a little periodical of his own devising entitled *NIB*. He enjoyed doing everything connected with *NIB*, even the advertising. Bonnard followed him in April with a baby singing the praises of a certain brand of baby's bottle in verses by Romain Coolus. Unfortunately, *NIB*—a slim prospectus immortalized by Lautrec, Bonnard, Vallotton and Jules Renard—had no more than three issues, sandwiched between *Paludes* and Mallarmé.

A snapshot from this period shows us Pierre Bonnard, a young man with a black beard, clutching a soft hat. He stands with two ladies whose dresses date them exactly, in what looks like a village street, perhaps Eragny. It was probably the same street that he painted in shades of blue and pinkish grey, peopling it with two dogs meeting.

It was this same silhouette of Bonnard that Vuillard sketched in at the left of his first version of a decorative panel he painted for Claude Anet between 1898 and 1936.

Once a week Madame Vuillard, a corsetière in the Rue Saint-Honoré, pushed the sewing machine into a corner and entertained her son's friends to dinner. As well as Bonnard, of whom she was specially fond although she teased him a great deal, there were Paul Percheron, son of the fashionable dressmaker Mélanie Percheron, and the gentle Paul Hermant, a delightful

WATER CARNIVAL AT HAMBURG, 1908-1912

but unfortunate composer. When the parents of Ker Roussel, Edouard's friend since the Lycée Condorcet, separated, Ker came to live with Madame Vuillard. Marie Vuillard, a timid girl in a woollen dress, used to bring in the soup-tureen, the *bœuf à la mode* and the *œufs à la neige* and clear the table. Roussel was good-looking; one day an embarrassed Vuillard advised his friend to go away from the house that had become almost his own : 'My sister is in love with you.' 'In that case,' Roussel chimed in, 'I shall marry her.' Marie Roussel was to remain like some calm shining vestal, her hair and her bodice tightly bound, silent and awestruck in her husband's presence. Other women desired and seduced him, attracted by the tawny eyes that made him look like a king of the jungle.

Bonnard and Vuillard did not address each other with the intimate 'tu'. Marie, as reserved as they, was to use the formal 'vous' to Roussel all her life.

Roussel's poetic but often obscure philoso-phical style made more impression on Bonnard than the theorems of Sérusier. Amused at first, then intent, Bonnard would wipe his glasses and his ironic gaze would become more and more penetrating.

'My dear Charles,' Pierre wrote to his brother, 'I am astonished that in your distant barracks you still take an interest in the Cirque Médrano. Yes, it still exists. I often go, it's just near where I live. I always enjoy the circus, and for one who goes alone, it has the advantage that the intervals are amusing. In the theatre they are

Illustration for Marie

THE CHERRY TART, 1908

Project for illustration for Le Cirque, pen drawing

unspeakable. One goes to the bar where the clowns drink. Then there are the stables where one can go to say hello to the horses and other beasts...'

Notice the white horse that carries the *Bareback Rider*. It may seem an unsteady sort of apparition now, but it is the same one that will appear to Bonnard half a century later, at the end of his career.

Bonnard's first one-man show took place at the beginning of January 1896, at the Durand-Ruel gallery; fifty works in the catalogue. Gustave Geffroy devoted a long article to Bonnard in *La Vie artistique*, comparing him with Vuillard, 'his friend and companion... there are obvious resemblances between the two artists... I also see important differences : Vuillard is more frank and direct in his use of colour, bolder in allowing his blues, reds and golds to burst into flower—and yet one can feel that he is melancholy by nature, that his thoughts are grave. Bonnard, on the other hand, is a grey painter. He loves the subtleties of violet, russet-brown, sombre tints; and yet in everything he sets down there is a charmingly individual malicious observation, a touch of impudent gaiety.'

This praise did not meet with the approval of Pissarro, despite that warty patriarch's normally indulgent nature. The old revolutionary dreamer wrote to his son Lucien Pissarro that he was horrified by the Bonnard pictures at the Durand-Ruel exhibition. 'He has failed miserably,' Pissarro declared, 'although Gustave Geffroy proclaims his triumphs in the press.' He added

RACES AT BOULOGNE, 1910

that 'every painter of any merit—Puvis, Degas, Renoir, Monet' (and himself) agreed in finding the work of the 'symbolist' Pierre Bonnard 'hideous in the extreme. What is more, the exhibition is a complete fiasco.'

Pissarro was to revise his judgement before three years had passed. In 1899 he wrote to his son on the occasion of Durand-Ruel's 'Tribute to Redon' exhibition: 'This young artist (Bonnard) will go far. He has a painter's eye.'

Signac, who had noted in his diary in 1893 that Bonnard's figures looked like rags, was also to have second thoughts.

Thadée Natanson, one of the first collectors of Bonnard's work and his friend from first to last, poured out his enthusiasm in a long article for *La Revue Blanche*. 'His colour,' he wrote, 'has infinite complexity, infinite variety. It plays on the muted notes of the background, bursts out almost stridently in sharp accents and harmonies, scatters highlights, a piece of ribbon, a buckle, a glove, a face, which arrange themselves in bouquets. The colours of flesh are accompanied and set off by nuances of blue porcelain, glasses, a sealed bottle gilded by a ray of sunlight. This gift has enabled him to triumph over the monochrome of greenery...'

In *La Revue Blanche* for 15 January, 1896, this praise of Bonnard appears between the leading article, which is about the death of Verlaine, and a major unpublished piece by Tolstoy on persecution in Russia.

A year later, at an exhibition at the Galerie Vollard in which Vuillard showed his *Good Samaritan* (a pastel which I later saw darken gradually on my father's wall), Bonnard showed seven pictures including *The Garden of the Moulin-Rouge*. Paris gardens at night with their milky gas-lamps; the illuminated sails of the red windmill turning in the shining wet Place Blanche.

Another of the seven pictures was *First Light in the Champs-Elysées*. Carriages on their way up to the Bois. Iron chairs lined up at the edge of the pavement. Birds at the ends of branches against a dappled sky. A light-coloured glove rests on the handle of a parasol.

In the summer of 1897 Bonnard painted a portrait of his friend Thadée in front of some chestnut trees in a 'monochrome of greenery' at Villeneuve. He loved the garden of Le Relais, the great courtyard where the stage coaches had once been harnessed, the rose-trees, the ivy-covered wall, and the virginia creeper which choked the stable doors.

Back from a bicycle-ride in the Yonne valley, Bonnard smiles and screws up his eyes against the light as he leans on his handlebars in the sandy bowling-alley. This photograph from an old album dates from long before I took my first steps at Villeneuve, but the hat, the short, coarse beard, the head bent a little forwards, the chest a little hollow, are just as I knew them later. I remember his hands, which were those of a workman, with thick, square, soft fingers, and which remained bluish-red all the year round, and his white teeth which all showed at once when he laughed. For a long time I believed that this photograph, like those which

THE NATANSON GIRLS, 1906-1910

show Renoir sitting on a bench with Misia, was taken on that bright September Sunday when Mallarmé's coffin was escorted by his friends from the little house at Valvins to the cemetery at Samoreau. But this was one of those faded images of the past which crumble to dust when exposed to the air, like long-buried garments. In reality, the day when Bonnard stood in his white pullover against the background of the chestnut trees was one year earlier than I had thought.

Photograph taken by Alfred Natanson (Alfred Athis)

'MARIE' AND 'L'INDOLENTE'

Illustration for Marie

In the foreground of a picture he painted at Le Cannet about 1925 stands a table bearing an inkwell, a post-office pen-rack, and a book. On the white paper cover the title stands out in black : MARIE.

Marie, a delightful love-story from the Danish, was illustrated by Bonnard for *La Revue Blanche* in 1897. Its author, Peter Nansen, has never been widely known in France, although Vallotton has preserved for us his round face with its astute look and well-trimmed moustache. *Marie* meant more to Bonnard than eighteen delicious drawings; in it he had found the fleeting grace of youth, which, even at thirty, his hand already traces with a touch of wistfulness. All his life, his eye and his brush were to keep this grace alive. In drawing Marie, Bonnard discovered femininity. He seized with the quickness of a poacher on its ephemeral, intangible qualities, never crushing a single petal. Marie taking off her straw hat, or sitting on the edge of her bed to do up her garter, Marie reading a letter from her beloved as a cat laps a bowl of milk, Marie in her virginal corsage, a froth of curls falling to reveal a youthful neck; thin arms along the line of two growing breasts; all the animal delicacy of a girl in love when her beauty is still hardly in flower.

The laughing *France-Champagne* poster on the street-corners had drawn the attention of Lautrec ; it was *Marie* that touched the heart of Renoir. The drawings delighted him and he wrote at once to Bonnard, whom he did not then know : 'You have a little note of charm, do not neglect it... it is a precious gift.'

Later, the ageing Renoir was to ask the astonished Bonnard to exchange a picture with him. Renoir was perhaps the first to sense not only that Bonnard was a great painter, but that he was to be the greatest painter of the twentieth century.

In March, 1899 the Nabis, along with Emile Bernard, Cross, Signac, Luce and a few others, paid tribute to Redon in a collective exhibition at the Galerie Durand-Ruel.

In the *Choses d'Art* column of *Le Temps* Thiébault-Sisson devoted an article to 'this curious exhibition.'

'There is some interest in following, in the first of these sub-groups, the evolution of the Symbolists of yesteryear. We recall the curiosity aroused, exactly eight years ago, by the first exhibition of this youthful group... like his friend Séruzier (*sic*) Paul Bonnard (*sic* again) showed signs of being more of a decorator...'

Why was the exhibition a tribute to Redon ?

The Nabis had taken to meeting for tea on certain fixed days at Odilon Redon's flat in the avenue de Wagram. Redon was a paternal figure, so modest (very unlike Gauguin) that the deference of his young colleagues rather intimidated him. He received his young visitors with an exquisite tact which excluded any idea of superiority. He spoke rather quietly, in his soft Bordeaux accent, and listened attentively. Redon at over fifty was not yet 'known', but to a being whose spiritual life belonged to the world of the unreal this must have mattered little.

Bonnard admired Redon profoundly : 'What strikes me most in his work is the conjunction of two almost opposite qualities : the content is pure and the expression mysterious.' Redon was more of a visionary than an observer; his genius never influenced Bonnard, who nevertheless continued to visit him frequently. Redon's grave profile of Bonnard, with its nuances from white to black, and Bonnard's *Portrait of Arï Redon* are precious tokens of what was, despite the gap between the two generations, a perfect friendship.

'Redon,' wrote Maurice Denis in *Théories*, 'tried to remain a painter, exclusively a painter, while translating into paint the lights and shadows of his imagination.'

Denis had already written in his diary for March 1898 (one year before the Durand-Ruel exhibition) : 'Do a picture of Redon in Vollard's shop with Vuillard, Bonnard etc., and Vollard.' This is the idea of the famous *Tribute to Cézanne* which Denis showed at the *Nationale* in 1901. At the Musée d'Art Moderne, where it can now be seen, all these young painters are to be identified, but it is to Redon that they are paying tribute. They stand in front of a picture by Cézanne, but all eyes are on Redon, who is wiping his glasses. They seem to be presenting

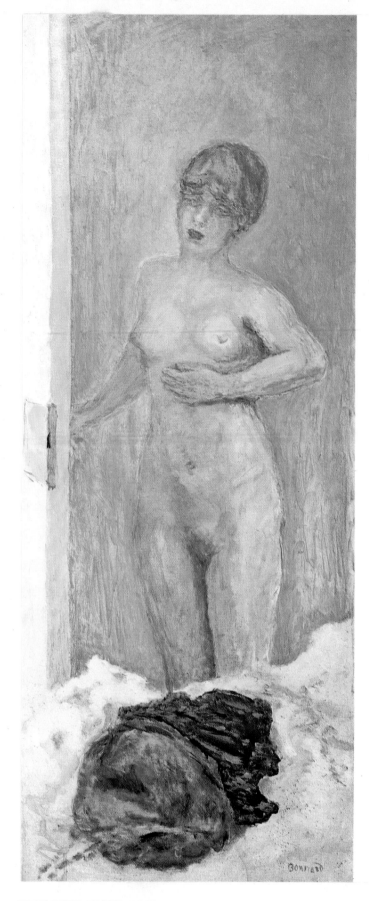

NUDE WITH TOQUE, 1911   NUDE WITH COVERLET, 1911   65

Picking Fruit, pen and brush drawing

the Cézanne still-life to him, the same still-life that Gauguin loved so much that he kept it with him even in the depths of his poverty. It appears in his *Portrait of Marie Henry.*

Vollard, an ape-like giant, holds on to one of the uprights of the easel, and Bonnard, with his little flat hat and his cane, has the serene curiosity of a true Parisian out to take the air.

But the countryside still called. His grandmother wrote : 'There will be masses of fruit and you can pick pears. The cow is in milk now and I am selling it to the neighbours at four sous a litre. This brings in quite a lot...'

When he arrived at Le Clos, Pierre wrote to his brother Charles : 'I hope you will get leave next Sunday and we shall all be together. The heat is extraordinary. Everyone bathes, the children in the pool in front of the house and the grown-ups in the tub. The children's pool is a charming sight.'

The Children in the Pool moved 'Uncle Pierre' to paint a picture in which astonishing symmetry is allied to the nuances of an affectionate fancy. Grass and water, blues and greens, naked children, a little lilac and pink...

From 1899, too, dates a picture that belonged to my younger uncle until my elder uncle bought it in a public sale. *L'Indolente*—I did not know its title—presided over the bedroom of Uncle Alexandre and Aunt Olga. This was a remote sanctuary I seldom visited. But the youngest of my cousins, girls a little older than myself, used to make use of their authority to

THE PROVENÇAL CARAFE, 1912-1915

give me any delicate missions that needed doing. On Sundays I was sent to beg a few coins from their mother to pay for rides on the roundabouts in the Champs-Elysées.

When my aunt was neither in the little drawing-room nor in the library, I had to go and knock at the door of this well-guarded bedroom. In the little ante-room a whole section of the wall was occupied by a redoubtable janissary in a black cape with a red scarf thrown back over it : *Aristide Bruant* by Lautrec.

I would hesitate for a moment, terrified at the thought of asking for money. When the distant voice of my aunt answered 'Come in!' I would enter and see her sitting with her back to me at her dressing-table near the window. On my right I could see a most surprising picture.

Across a large, disordered bed lay a naked lady, her hair in disarray, one leg hanging down, resting but clearly not asleep. I was so timid of looking at her that I did not make out the plaster pipe on the bedside table nor the cat, nestling close to her shoulder, which blended with the harmonies of light and dark, yellow, blue, green and blackish brown that confused my eye.

Aunt Olga teased me for my boldness—she could not hear my pounding heart!—and gave me two francs which my cousins, posted outside in the gallery, promptly took away from me on the pretext that pickpockets might steal them. They had several rides on the roundabout, and then sucked enormous barley-sugars in front of me. It was all quite natural : I was the smallest.

Illustration for Marie

Right : page from Parallèlement

Oui, ma vague, sois orgueilleuse,
Car radieuse ou sourcilleuse,
Je suis ton vaincu, tu m'as tien :
Tu me roules comme la vague
Dans un délice bien païen,
Et tu n'es pas déjà si vague!

70   *The Little Square, pencil drawing*

THE TUILERIES GARDENS, 1912

But today, *L'Indolente*, even seen in a photograph, conjures up for me all the anguish and the melancholy of a child scared by adult mysteries she cannot imagine.

The girl who lies

> *presque nue*
> *Sur un canapé noir*
> *Dans un jaune boudoir...*

has exactly the same pose as *L'Indolente*; she appears in *Parallèlement*, a happy encounter in a hundred and ten pink-sanguine lithographs between Bonnard and Verlaine, in which the drawings defy the laws of typography to twine themselves amorously round the text.

This exquisite book, published in 1900 by Vollard, made a curious entry into the world. Vollard had had it printed at the Imprimerie Nationale, but he was unaware that certain passages of *Parallèlement* had been condemned by the courts. The day after the book came out, Vollard was visited by a Ministry official who said 'It is not fitting that a book which has been condemned as tending to corrupt public morals should be republished in a cover bearing the emblem of the Republic, and with a title page bearing the inscription "by special permission of the Minister of Justice".'

Echoes of this incident even reached the Chamber of Deputies, but all was finally settled. For the unsold copies (the others became extremely rare collectors' pieces) Bonnard designed a new cover.

This farcical episode had no effect on sales. Bonnard's *Parallèlement* had no success at the time of publication except with a few German bibliophiles.

The charm of these stylized caprices belongs to a lost spring and Bonnard left them behind with the dying century, along with his acidulous arabesques, his sombre figures, his brown faces with black hair in a copper-coloured light. Copper grapes, apples sliced open to show a bluish cut surface, still-life paintings heavy with autumnal domesticity and sprinkled lightly with russet. Until Bonnard launched on his first blazing fanfares of colour, his light remained subdued, as if filtered by a Paris mist.

In the Rue Saint-Florentin, in the halo of one of those yellow-shaded lamps that Vuillard also painted, Misia, the wife of his friend Thadée, spreads out a pattern on the table. Her skilled hands give it the style of tomorrow: 1900.

In the list of contents of *La Revue Blanche* for 15 May 1900: Chapter XIV of Mirbeau's *Journal d'une Femme de Chambre*, and book reviews by André Gide who writes on *The War of the Worlds* and *The Light that Failed*. 'Messrs Wells and Kipling, young though they are, have inherited much of the popularity of Stevenson.'

In the same issue, an article by Thadée Natanson on *Intelligent Painters*, among whose number 'only Messrs Bonnard, Maurice Denis, Ibels, Ranson, Roussel, Sérusier, Vallotton and Vuillard could strictly be included.'

AVENUE DU BOIS DE BOULOGNE, 1912-1914   73

Little Girl with Dog, pen drawing

In the Japanese theatre at the *Exposition universelle*, Mme Sada Yacco twisted her hands and wailed the history of the geisha and the samurai.

At the Porte Dauphine, the green and yellow *art nouveau* entrance to the metropolitan railways bore an awning with dragonfly wings. '. . . There is the *métro*,' wrote Pierre to his grandmother, 'It amuses me to see the passengers piled together, and there are often pretty faces that I draw from memory in the evenings in my notebook. . .'

Bonnard's Paris is not the harrowing, gloomy place that Utrillo peopled with broad-bottomed dummies. It is the light-footed, living Paris caricatured by later and sadder generations, who took the comic soldier and the *pétomane* as representatives of the age.

Paris, with its café terraces, its gas-lamps, its little milliners ('a painter should judge as a milliner judges the hat she makes,' Bonnard was to say in his old age).

Paris in fine weather and in the rain. Wines and Spirits, *Compagnie Générale des Omnibus*. Sacré-Cœur. Great square baskets, crammed with mimosa, against the thighs of flower-girls. The Paris bridges where Bonnard never tired of opening his soul to the sky, its flakes of silver cloud, its violet immensity, and where, like Fouquet in the *Book of Hours* of Etienne Chevalier, he discovered the city.

Place Blanche. Behind the low building of the restaurant for weddings and banquets rises a blank wall dedicated to *Suprême Pernot* biscuits. Children in capes and galoshes still reign supreme

Etching for Dingo

in the roadway, which carries at most one or two fiacres and the white horses of a delivery-van.

Place Blanche, Place Clichy; the Parisian landscape seen through a window by which a young woman sits. Paris from above, or Paris from a loiterer's eye view. For Easter the women put bunches of brilliant cherries on their straw hats, and poppies on the hats of their little girls.

Les Parisiennes, sketch

MARTHE

Portrait of a Lady,
project for an engraving, pen drawing

Girls, some wearing capes, some hatless, some wearing straw boaters, elegant little working-girls carrying hat-boxes, loaves of bread, muffs, or little dogs that must not dirty their paws : all these fleeting outlines Pierre captured, distorted slightly and brought to life. 'Often it is the improbable that is true,' he was to say.

One of these passing figures became his companion for life and never lost the look she had when he first saw her.

Bonnard met Marthe in 1894; she was sixteen years old.

On the Boulevard Haussmann, where the steam-tram, that dark juggernaut, advanced with a grinding of metal while the driver rang the bell, Pierre helped Marthe across the road.

On the corner of the Rue Pasquier was a shop which supplied artificial flowers for funerals. There, just opposite the Chapelle Expiatoire whose bulk covers tumbril-loads of victims of the guillotine, Maria Boursin, alias Marthe de Méligny, threaded on to iron wires the tiny translucent pearls used in funeral wreaths. With her pale hair and acid, inexpressive eyes, 'Marthe de Méligny'—heaven knows why she chose the name of a courtesan for herself—looked as Ophelia might have looked if she had turned *midinette*. She never spoke of her family, to Pierre

or anyone else, and no-one ever knew where she came from.

She always seemed to be staving off some illness or other—she had a weak chest, or perhaps tubercular laryngitis—and a hoarse, breathless voice. I remember her twenty years later, a touchy elf dressed in a wild assortment of colours, as she gruffly declared to my mother that she was 'ravaged'. Her speech was weirdly savage and harsh. Marthe, bird-like in her garish plumage, unstable save in love, touched the heart of my mother, always sensitive to the anguish of those who are condemned by their own singularity.

Marthe and Pierre were a strangely-matched couple; although they changed with age, they never aged. He looked after her, feared her, put up with her, loved her : she caused him endless worry and distress, but she was part of him; her presence was at the heart of all his work.

We see Marthe at table, in the garden, in her bedroom, nibbling, scrubbing herself, naked or in the strangest garb—but always Marthe. And it is always the charming body of her youth that he substitutes, over the years, for that which time has caused to fade. Marthe resting at Le Cannet in the rainbow of her bathtub always remains *L'Indolente* as she was at the height of her beauty. He renews her beauty just as nature renews the leaves every spring.

Pierre and Marthe were poor together. They went without things and did not complain—

Nude, pen drawing

Etching for Sainte Monique

THE POPPIES, 1914

except perhaps a little to each other; they were as envious as children of the luxuries others could afford. Pierre, who was never to lose his thrifty habits, detested money, which seemed to him to produce nothing but complications. Shut in together in their narrow, vagabond existence, they shared a fondness for discomfort. Pierre Bonnard's luxury is all in his painting. And if he kept his accounts with scrupulous fairness both to others and to himself, it was because he could remember the days when he had to go short. He hated all waste and husbanded his time even more carefully than his income.

Marthe never forgot the difficulties of the early days. Years later she said to Annette, Roussel's daughter, 'I'm worried... I know that Pierre's pictures are selling well, but is it going to last? It's a specialized sort of painting...'

They used to eat great thick steaks, almost raw—this was fortifying for Marthe. Like any good bourgeois housewife, she always carved the maid's portion and put it on one side.

Just before the turn of the century, Pierre and Marthe rented a tiny cottage for the summer at Montval, between Mareil and Marly. Maurice Denis lived at Saint-Germain, the Roussels at L'Etang-la-Ville. The road from Montval to Marly rises high enough to see the church tower at L'Etang and, in the background, the dark green swell of the forest.

All this Vuillard noticed when he walked with Bonnard to see Ker and Marie Roussel, and he painted it on two panels for the dining-room of my grandfather Natanson. Those panels were

one day to play a part in the day-dreams of a little girl who was never hungry and who hated spinach.

I can remember trees and ridges, slate-roofed steeples, the white of a little house—perhaps it was Bonnard's—against the dense greenery, and the woman leaning out of a window to water her potted geraniums.

The next summer, Pierre and Marthe took up residence at L'Etang-la-Ville with Roussel's mother, a shock-haired old eccentric who was always gesticulating with her long thin arms or running after her goat. She did not get on badly with Marthe, in spite of frequent shrill quarrels. The hens pecked around everywhere. This was the rustic atmosphere that Bonnard was to transmute into Greek pastoral. *Daphnis et Chloé* was published by Vollard in 1902.

'One day', Vollard writes, 'I saw Bonnard kneading a piece of bread between his fingers. It gradually took the shape of a little dog. "Bonnard", I said, "isn't that sculpture? Why don't you do me some statuettes?"

'Bonnard did not say no, and after a few experiments he started work on a large centre-piece. One afternoon the sound of someone hammering metal could be heard in the base-ment of my shop. It was Bonnard beating his bronze.'

The astonishing work that Vollard exhibited in 1902 may now be seen at the Musée d'Art

Two pages from Daphnis et Chloé, black and white lithographs

telle qu'étoit Chloé, mais même à lui chevrier.
Ils ne purent donc la nuit suivante reposer non
plus que l'autre, et n'eurent ailleurs la pensée
qu'à remémorer ce qu'ils avoient fait, et regretter
ce qu'ils avoient omis à faire, disant ainsi en eux-
mêmes : «Nous nous sommes baisés, et de rien

conque l'eût vue en tel état n'eût point fait doute d'affirmer par serment qu'elle n'étoit point fille de Dryas, lequel toutefois étoit à table comme les autres avec sa femme Napé, et Lamon et Myrtale aussi, tous quatre sur un même lit.

TEA, 1916

Moderne : it is an oval, with tangled figures clustering round the grassy outline of a pool represented by a mirror.

'A curious evening at Vollard's,' wrote Maurice Denis in his diary on 28 October, 1903, 'with Marthe (Marthe Denis), Dierx, the Redons, Bonnard, André, Mme Cornillac, and some lesbian women. The dinner was exotic and highly seasoned, and by the end of the evening conversation had taken a decidedly ribald turn.'

It was another dinner-party of the same kind, held in Vollard's cellar at about the same time, that Bonnard made into a ferocious painting in which some have identified Forain in the midst of the crowd of middle-aged men and beplumed young persons. Vollard, his napkin tucked into his collar, is in the act of raising a bottle of burgundy.

In his shop in the Rue Laffitte, piled high with Cézannes and Van Goghs, Vollard used to light a lamp at dusk and pretend to sleep in order to hear the opinions of connoisseurs about the young painters whose success he was anxious to share. Renoir and Degas were often there; and there is a little Bonnard drawing which shows Pissarro, who was to die so poor, smiling amid the chaos of Vollard's shop.

About 1904 Bonnard did a *Portrait of Vollard* showing his head shaped like an avocado pear, with one drooping eye. Vollard was a ponderous clown with a relaxed, Creole way of speaking; but while people were laughing at him, he was making careful notes of the replies to his repeated question 'Tell me, what do you think

Nude Washing her Foot, pen drawing

of . . . ?' and hoarding a mass of treasures in his basement.

In the Petit-Palais there is another portrait of Vollard, done fifteen years later. Bonnard shows him sitting sideways on a chair amid piles of pictures. He looks like a sad gorilla, holding between his enormous hands a kitten with a red ribbon round its neck. This is the same Vollard who used to appear at Cabourg in a light-brown suit and hand Mme de Galea down from her limousine. She was a mauve apparition in a cloud of muslin and tulle, smiling in the midst of her frills and flounces, with her face just a trifle flushed, like all those blonde beauties who had to reconcile a rich diet and a narrow waist.

NUDE WASHING HER FOOT IN THE BATH, 1920-1922

SELF-PORTRAIT WITH BEARD, 1920-1925

'I shall be glad to see some lucerne again and smell the new-mown hay when I arrive...'

The Ile-de-France did not make Bonnard forget his beloved Dauphiné. Every spring and most autumns, he made his way back to Le Clos. He repeated the walks he had taken in his holidays from school: Lake Paladin, La Côte-Saint-André (Berlioz' birthplace), La Tour-du-Pin. A little further afield lay Brangues. 'This magnificent piece of country... more than a heritage, a conquest... a vocation...' as Claudel was to call the ground where he now lies buried.

At Le Grand-Lemps there is the Rue du Devin, the Rue du Derrière and the Place aux Cochons.

Le Clos itself was sold in April 1929 by Jean, the eldest of the Terrasse boys, to the directors

STANDING NUDE, 1922-1930

Illustration for Le Prométhée mal enchaîné

of a neighbouring weaving-mill. Maître Pinel, the notary, recorded at the time that it was 'a property... comprising a dwelling-house with four rooms on the ground floor, four rooms on the first floor, two attic rooms and an underground cellar, also a barn, a stable, a coach-house, and a gardener's dwelling, the whole in a poor state of repair, with a courtyard, a fountain delivering one litre of water per minute, a flower-garden, a kitchen-garden, a field and a paddock, the whole covering an area of approximately two hectares, ten ares...'

When the present owners bought the now 'horribly dilapidated' house (no doubt the scattered members of the family had not been near it for years), they burned a number of stiff, dry, rolled-up canvases someone had found in a corner, as well as an old screen with flowers painted on it, signed P. B. ...

The dark mahogany Pleyel piano which belonged to Claude Terrasse is still there. So are the magnificent trees; just in front of the terrace stands the huge pine under which Bonnard used to sit. Vivette used to climb into its branches.

In the village lives Laïa, as everyone called the cook Maria Didier. She will be a hundred years old in 1965. Laïa does not remember much, and she repeats herself a great deal, but there is one thing she is consistent about.

'Such a nice family! I have never known such a nice family. M. Terrasse was always gay and laughing. M. Pierre never stopped painting. His paintings looked a bit funny but he was such a nice boy, so well brought up. He only came

WOMAN IN AN INTERIOR, 1925

93

in the holidays. The children had a donkey called Trotty, and Didier—my husband—used to teach them to ride a bicycle on the paths. I was a good cook. They even got me the *cordon bleu*. Mme Bonnard wanted butter in everything, but M. Pierre didn't mind what he ate... they were a nice family. I always think about them when I'm ill... They're all dead now. Mme Bonnard is in the cemetery here. I put a pine-branch on her coffin just as she wanted.'

In Bonnard's *L'Après-midi bourgeoise*, the blank façade of today, with its dead wistaria, lives again... The time is the beginning of the century. Bonnard's family stands in front of the house; all in shades of green and light bluish-grey. After selling this picture to the Bernheims, the artist decided that it was too green; so he painted it again, greener than ever. This second version is now in Munich. On the bench sit Claude Terrasse and his son Jean; at Claude's feet the bitch Mouche that Bonnard had bought as a puppy from a peasant and brought back from the mountains in his waistcoat pocket. In an armchair sits Mme Prudhomme, with her comfortable bosom, and at her side Charles Terrasse, her godson, Jean's brother. Andrée Terrasse bends over a playful kitten in the same pose that appears in the Japanese-flavoured works of ten years before. On the right, in an angler's hat, stands the corpulent, pipe-smoking figure of M. Prudhomme, archivist of the department of the Isère, and godfather of little Charles. Robert, the third Terrasse boy—the round-cheeked baby seen in many of Bonnard's pic-

tures—sits by the pool that now no longer exists. In the foreground Vivette, the spoilt youngest child of the family, is being held upright by her nurse. In the window can be seen Renée Terrasse, the rational big sister who always remembers to say to the others 'Have you washed your hands?' The two other children are 'supernumeraries' (never leave a gap). The laurels in tubs are magnificent; so is the orange-tree and the virginia creeper. At the top of the steps, Mme Bonnard-Mertzdorff, the mother of Pierre and Andrée is returning to her drawing-room.

In homespun and in richer fabrics draped,
Through her lorgnette Madame Bonnard-Mertzdorff
Seeking a footman-majordomo-cook
Able to milk and pick the apples too.

as Franc-Nohain wrote.

His sons, Jaboune and Claude Dauphin, also remember her; they spent the first summer of the Great War at Le Clos with their friends the Terrasse children. 'She was an enormous woman in black with a black, ruched bonnet. She seemed to live on butter. She ate butter with everything, pursing her lips with relish to suck it in. She put it into her breakfast coffee with her knife. The butter dish which always stood on the check tablecloth, and appears in many of her son's pictures, had to be refilled for her every day. People laughed at her a little; she was a very charming woman who surely died (at an advanced age) of an excess of cholesterol.'

WOMAN AT WASH-STAND,
1925

My Companions, project for illustration for Histoires naturelles

The patriarch of the Bonnard dogs was the dachshund Fachol. His rat's tail had been broken in an accident and the end dangled as if about to come off.

In the village, on the spot where a chain-store now stands, was the Café Brosse, where Terrasse and Jarry, who had become something of a hanger-on, would drink their *picon-citron* before dinner. Terrasse could carry his aperitifs quite well, but Jarry sometimes passed out before they got home. One morning they found him in the rabbit-hutch. When they cut off his supplies of drink he drank liquid dentifrice.

In 1904, Bonnard illustrated a new Flammarion edition of Jules Renard's *Histoires naturelles*, with animals from Le Grand-Lemps, Montval, L'Etang-la-Ville, the Bois de Boulogne, everywhere.

44 Rue du Rocher, the building where the Renard family lived: a little corner of the Paris of Balzac and Corot. I have a distant memory of the black door at the top of three steps; a lodge for the *concierge* crammed with children who were always having whooping cough or coming home from the elementary school in their aprons; the musty smell of the dark staircase hung with red-patterned hessian, the narrow landing, the brass bell. The immaculate apartment with its creaking parquet floors was pervaded by a smell of cleanliness. The furniture was sparse and simple. In the small, light dining-room the chairs stood by the wall and there was a white china swan on the green-covered table: a *jardinière* with no flowers in it. In Jules

The Cat, brush drawing for Histoires naturelles 97

Renard's study there was one single 'decorative' object, a present from the Rostands. It is the bat from the *Histoires naturelles*, made of beaten metal with a round green glass window for a stomach.

This modest apartment, lovingly cared for, did not succeed even in being ugly. Any idea of taste—to say nothing of art—was quite foreign to the meticulous Renard. So it is not very surprising that this wonderful observer, who worked in direct contact with reality, did not really appreciate the charm of Bonnard's art.

He had not appreciated Lautrec or Vallotton as illustrators either. His diary contains no mention of Bonnard. Just after the Flammarion edition came out, he added this postscript to a letter to Paul Cornu: 'Come and collect your copy of the illustrated *Histoires naturelles*.' No mention of the artist's name. Only in a letter to my father dated 11 October 1906 did he volunteer the following tribute: 'Yes, Bonnard has something...'

'The eye acts like a fishing net; images imprint themselves in it of their own accord' writes Renard. Bonnard's eyes are traps too, but his memory strips the images and then clothes them more richly. He turns pumpkins into coaches.

Here and there in the Rue Laffitte, a succession of group exhibitions took place. Bonnard continued to show his work at the *Salon des Indépendants* and the *Salon d'Automne*. He sent work

The Cock and the Hen, brush drawings for Histoires naturelles

Nude Dressing, brush drawing

off to Brussels, Berlin, Prague. In 1906 he had a one-man exhibition at the Bernheim-Jeune gallery.

Marthe lies on her *chaise-longue*, or strokes the dog Black before she goes out, or reads the future in a pack of cards. In her chemise, she takes off her shoes and stockings. A draught-board, or a veil of Genoese lace behind her face or at the foot of the bed are no longer enough to indicate the place; henceforth she is surrounded by the elements of her personal 'landscape'. Doors stand open and we enter the endless succession of intimate early-mornings viewed against the light.

A scrap of linoleum in front of the galvanized-iron tub becomes a magic carpet leading us to the flowery secret of the lace curtains, the little triple mirror, the jug and basin. The glass in a bamboo frame reflects the charming ritual of the wash-stand in all its easy coquetry.

At about the same time Bonnard was painting portraits of a number of very different sitters. Misia on her elegant *canapé* has the radiance of Watteau's best work. A setting of subtle elegance, a vase of roses, mirrors that catch the light, all her silken, petulant ease. Bonnard mocks this magnificence with the hand of a master.

Misia, with her Slavonic wiles, her feline charm, her extravagance and her vast appetite for money, had by then reached her third husband, Alfred Edwards.

In spite of her pathological horror of 'society', which perhaps concealed a suppressed desire to

99

The Two Friends, pen drawing, illustration for Parallèlement

Right : At the Casino, pencil and charcoal drawing

be in it, Marthe was attracted by Misia's unceremonious, rather lordly kindness, her way of laughing, her breathtaking chic, her inborn eccentricity. All this made a deep impression on one who, as a jealous working-girl, had naively chosen for herself the name of Marthe de Méligny.

It is not at all surprising that Vuillard should have been in love with Misia, more so even than his friends; she was their communal muse. But children do not of course have any idea of the dreams, the follies and the tears of grown-up persons.

101

Monsieur Vuillard, as I knew him—indulgent, solicitous, calm, but subject to outbursts of rage—was exactly the saint in black boots that Bonnard painted, with his ready-made clothes from 'La Belle Jardinière', his white collar and slender necktie, his pink baldness, his grave but lively eye. I can also remember the clean, tawny smell of his beard when one kissed him. He had a long nose which was later to be marked with red veins; he used to rub it with his fingers as if he wanted to make it even longer and thinner than it was.

My father used to read Andersen's fairy-tales to me as I sat for my portrait by Vuillard. All the dark words I heard then, *penury, coffin, shadow, witch,* brought a lump to my throat: Death and the Angel blending in a legendary gloom.

One family group is the portrait of Josse and Gaston Bernheim (the Bernheim-Jeune brothers) with their wives who were sisters. Bonnard has them sitting in full evening-dress in a box at the theatre. The time is 1908. One of the brothers is at the back, and the other is standing up, so that all his head except the chin is out of the picture. The attractive blonde woman on the left is Suzanne, Gaston's wife, who did not like the way Bonnard had distorted her arm in the picture. 'Faults sometimes give life to a picture', Bonnard told her. On the right of this superbly audacious piece of composition sits the figure of Mathilde, a black and white jewel.

Marthe did not like Suzanne and Mathilde, 'those Bernheim women', beautiful, rich, healthy,

charming *mondaines*, with their rather conventional elegance. Bonnard himself had a high regard for the two brothers, who treated him very considerately. They were successful, happy, and not at all mercenary. It was their brother-in-law, Félix Vallotton, who had introduced Bonnard to them a little before 1900. Their financial understanding with Bonnard (they had first refusal of all his pictures) was reached in 1904. It was never put into writing, and it lasted through nearly forty years of mutual trust. He deposited all his earnings with them and they took care of all his bills. At the time of the financial crisis of 1930 they had charge of such a large sum belonging to him that the responsibility made them nervous and they had to beg Bonnard to choose—for the first time in his life—a real bank. From that time forth they made periodic transfers of money into his account. On receiving each of these, Bonnard would write to them on a slip of paper: 'Money received, best wishes, Pierre'. To this arrangement posterity owes a delightful drawing which Bonnard did on the back of a bank-statement, one day when he was waiting to see the cashier. It is now part of the Carle Dreyfus bequest in the Louvre.

Since 1907 France Ranson, the 'Light of the Temple' had directed the Académie Ranson, which was to have a great influence on the painting of the younger generation over the next twenty years.

When she was widowed in 1909, the Nabis rallied round to help her. Every Saturday morning, Maurice Denis used to come in from Saint-

Germain to the Academy in the Rue Joseph-Bara to look at students' work. The young artists listened in attentive silence as the cherubic,

his long white beard and hair, Sérusier, the painter of Breton girls spinning wool in vast, dingy, secret forests, bore an exact if premature

Sketch for The Sea Trip, pen drawing

goateed figure of the author of *Théories* moved from easel to easel, delivering his precise critical judgements. Sérusier, too, indulged his pedagogic propensities: he later took pride in claiming a distant link with Cubism by virtue of the fact that he had once taught La Fresnaye. With

resemblance to the popular image of God the Father. At the beginning of the age of hysteria he was still innocently reproving those who refused to crush their spontaneity by using the

105

'golden number' to determine their colour-combinations. And docile young ladies persisted in their attempts to create desiccated still-lifes by following the 'holy measures'.

Vuillard's unaffected modesty prevented him from setting up as a professor. When he visited the Académie Ranson, it was to confess, weighed down with scruples, that he was still a learner

Sketch for The Arbour at Cannes, pencil drawing

Roussel's contribution was his Olympian fancy. Standing-in at short notice for Maurice Denis, he surprised and then delighted the students by reading them some of Baudelaire's art-criticism.

himself. He always found something 'encouraging' in the work submitted to him.

Bonnard, on the rare occasions when he appeared, looked with interest at the tentative

THE HARBOUR AT CANNES, 1926

THE SAUCEPANS, 1930

paintings and drawings of the students, but prudently avoided asserting himself. One day when he did give in to the temptation to give some advice to a young artist, he became distressed and said to his friend Jacques Rodrigues on the way out: 'I won't do it again. I never know which of us is right.'

Vallotton used to come to see us less often than the others, but the impression he made on me was all the stronger. He was an excellent teacher and had many pupils. He chose his words very carefully, and his voice retained something of a Swiss lilt, just as his eyes had something of the chill of a mountain lake when the north wind is blowing. Under his Calvinist exterior lurked a curious, Ingresque sensuality. Young women were intrigued, perhaps disturbed by him.

He was an admirable wood-engraver, destined by Nature to be the illustrator of *La Famille Lepic* and *Poil de Carotte*, but his painting was rather stiff and rigid, with its cruel lines and its harsh fanfare of satin. I am thinking of the portraits he did of my parents, especially my mother, her hair frighteningly black, in an aggressively-coloured *déshabillé*. Framed side-by-side in this way, father and mother scared us.

The portrait of Uncle Thadée that Vallotton had painted at Villeneuve as long ago as 1897 (the same year as Bonnard) was, although austere, a more pleasing likeness. It was composed like a Primitive to gladden the heart of Douanier Rousseau. Vallotton had a neat profile, short, colourless hair, and, in his youth, a little beard. He was the husband of Mme Rodrigues, Gabrielle, the dark, raucous-voiced sister of the Bernheim-Jeune brothers.

They lived in the Rue des Belles-Feuilles, already sadly bare. There, in their first-floor apartment in a quiet little hotel, I had a doll's tea party once with a very dark, nice little girl called Madeleine.

Vallotton was an Expressionist of a bitter, perhaps tormented, kind. In private life he was a good husband and an excellent father to his wife's children, who adored him. People said he was a miser, insanely obsessed with tidiness. In his youth in Paris he had been very poor and lived in a garret. I remember that he had a sort of cold charm, with a hint of possible demonic flashes.

In the last days of his life, Vallotton suddenly said out aloud : 'Bonnard—he was the first of us all!'

Bonnard loved nothing so much as excursions —on a bicycle, on foot, in a car—and his excursions and short journeys run like a thread through all his work. Always alert, he records in a hasty scrawl and filters the result in his memory. 'See the object once or a thousand times'. Once was enough on his journeys through Belgium, Holland, Germany; memories of them—gay, caustic, sly, affectionate, sometimes savage— lighten the pages of *La 628-E 8* and the splenetic words of Octave Mirbeau.

Belgian customs men, a chauffeur in buckskin, breakdowns (in period), motoring coats, little Parisian faces. Fearsome types : even the Kaiser. Canals and rivers; the inky blackness of mining districts; the great ports of Flanders and the Baltic with their negroes and their street-girls. Sailors, tulips, cathedrals. Castles perched above the Rhine. The charm of Bonnard's animals standing by roads deep with ruts. He saw everything and his brush makes us see it too.

In 1909, George Besson sat for a portrait by Bonnard, whom he hardly knew at the time.

'One May morning I arrived in his studio, a cell in a former monastery in the Rue de Douai. He seated me in an old armchair in front of a yellow door. He rubbed his hands in an energetic gesture that has remained with him, and started on my portrait. As he painted he smoked his pipe and crunched pralines that he took from a little paper bag on top of a rusty little round-topped stove.'

Three years later, in Besson's own apartment, Bonnard painted from his own sketches *La Place Clichy*, a picture that has been seen at the Louvre. The inside of a café sun-blind, the syphon twisted on its table, the crimson profile of the waiter. The fiery ears of corn, the vermilion posies, the tufts of feathers on the hats of passing women; the light-coloured roadway, the old façades splashed with colour, all these things belong to the joyous truth of Bonnard's own fantastic Paris.

There was a rather rickety green motor-car that Bonnard felt the need, in 1922, to rejuvenate. He added a few touches of lemon yellow to turn it into the Lorraine-Dietrich of his dreams.

Félix Fénéon, who had been the *'anar'* of the *'Procès des Trente'* and then secretary of *La Revue Blanche* where he had come to love Bonnard's work, became artistic director-dealer-*éminence grise* to the Bernheim-Jeune brothers. Since 1900 they had been installed on the Boulevard de la Madeleine, on the site of the present Madelios store.

Fénéon was an enigmatic sort of person; with his stringy beard and his clear eyes he looked like an apostolic goat. He examined everything with the minuteness of an expert accountant. Fénéon's situation, as a cultivated critic turned cunning salesman, amused Pierre a great deal. There was an entrance from the Boulevard and a little door in the Rue Richepanse. The gallery.

Illustrations for La 628-E 8

Right : Mediterranean Landscape, pencil drawing

111

Bonnard

was reached down a narrow passageway with, I think, yellow ochre walls. I used to accompany my father, holding his hand, when he went to look at the pictures and chat to Fénéon. This was at the period when there was a succession of small Bonnard exhibitions at the Bernheim gallery. I have found catalogues dated 1909, 1910 and 1911. Bonnard always showed recent works and it is possible to watch the Terrasse children grow, as they sit round the family table at Le Grand-Lemps or play piano duets. In another picture, a nude lies stretched on the pink *canapé*. The same woman ties up her hair with a ribbon. *La Sieste* seems an *Indolente* in reverse. In the Tuileries the foliage of great trees grows thick. On a chilly spring morning the light shines in on newly-washed flesh. Paris is still foggy. Clouds pile up above the Seine at Vernon. Then there was *La Petite Rue* which Vuillard loved and which Bonnard gave him. It can be seen in *The Room of Madame Vuillard*, above the sofa, where Vuillard also hung *Marthe and her Dog, Black*. A young woman in a hurry, carrying a cardboard box, walks quickly down a little street. In the background, in front of the oyster-seller, one of the first motor-buses goes past: they were yellow and

went from Batignolles to the Jardin des Plantes.

One day, quite casually, Fénéon said to Bonnard, 'You know, your Paris street-scenes are very popular...' Bonnard decided there and then to paint no more of them. He always feared vanity and the pitfalls of success.

Bonnard painted a portrait of my four cousins to which I think I owe my memory of what they were then. It must be because of this picture that I seem to remember their green dresses, Bollia's necklace, and her white collar. In the picture, Marcelle, the youngest of the four girls, who was four years older than I, is trying to hold the fox terrier. I forget its name, but not the name of the poodle, Czarna, which I knew as a poor old animal that never stirred from its cushion in the linen-room.

Evelyn's hair-ribbon, Geo's hair, the lock of a white cupboard, the blue music manuscript book, a lowered eyelid, a finger held up, the wet nose of a young dog, Bonnard's delicate touch gives them for ever the aspect of a single moment in time. Curiously, this recalls other images long forgotten : the cups at nursery teatime, the gravel of a minute garden paved with ivy, and the sun in the Avenue du Bois de Boulogne.

Left : Nude with Chair, crayon drawing

114   THE MOLE AT SAINT-TROPEZ, 1912

THE SOUTH

Illustration for La 628-E 8

'Dear Mother... I allowed myself to be tempted by an invitation from Paul Simon who insisted on my spending a few days in his house by the Mediterranean. The South was a very alluring idea, and when I got here it was like something out of the Arabian Nights. The sea, the yellow walls, the reflections as full of colour as the light. After a fragrant mid-day meal we went to call on some neighbours and I had the vision of a very dark girl in a pink dress down to her feet with an enormous blue parrakeet, uncaged, against the yellow, red and green background. I am now discovering the pebbles, the little walls, the olive-trees and the oaks...'

It is easy to guess the effect of this revelation on Bonnard's palette. He made his first essays in violence, drenching forms in colour.

In the following year, 1911, his Bernheim-Jeune exhibition was to include three decorative panels—*Méditerranée*—for the Moscow collector Ivan Morozov. But the letter to his mother ends with the words : 'I think I shall soon be longing for the green grass and the cows.'

In 1912 he settled at Vernonet, near Vernon, in a house called Ma Roulotte.

He had come there by way of Villennes and Médan as well as Vernouillet, where he had lived in the Maison des Carrières, a peasant hotel perched above a grassy ravine.

Ma Roulotte was a long, narrow, crooked house with flimsy walls and a wooden balcony, sheltering under a hill. The terrace looked out

landscape, with a changing sky: Bonnard suffused it all with the southern light that had revealed him to himself. *The Open Door* and *Dining-room in the Country* open on to a countryside that is a vision of Paradise.

The Tug, drawing for La 628-E 8

over a little wilderness of a garden which fell away to an arm of the Seine where a boat was moored.

When Bonnard was digging or watering his little garden, as he loved to do, he could look out and see the poplars shimmering in the distance, the willows waving, and the fields gleaming like gold. The river glittered through a tangle of branches. A tug passed. A gentle

The war came, and Bonnard, isolated, turned in upon himself. Marthe was almost always either ill or preoccupied with her own health.

At Saint Germain, where they now spent most of their time, and on his visits to the south, Bonnard did more thinking than he had ever done. He began to have doubts, to feel that he had never known how to paint or draw. After severe inner conflicts, his conclusion was that

THE SEINE, 1928-1930

he must start again from the beginning. One day he confessed to Charles Terrasse: 'I have gone back to school. I wanted to forget all the things I knew and know. I want to learn the things I don't know. I am going back to first principles, back to the a b c... and I mistrust myself, I mistrust everything that used to fascinate me, including the colours that excite you so much...'

It was some time before Bonnard was able to say to his nephew: 'I think I know now what it was. I was obsessed by colour. Almost without knowing it, I was sacrificing form. But form is real, it is impossible to do away with it in this

118   VASE OF ANEMONES AND EMPTY VASES, *c.*1933

PROVENÇAL JUG WITH FLOWERS, c.1931

119

arbitrary way. So I shall have to study drawing... I draw all the time. And after drawing comes composition, which should be an equilibrium. A picture that is well composed is half done...'

Bonnard began to perceive his universe with a more and more intent eye. Marthe, with her floating veils, may still remain a shadow next to the dark little dog in the stern of the boat, but the nudes are firmer and more rounded, and the expressions on the young girls' faces have an intensity which looks forward to the admirable *Portrait of Mme Pierre Bonnard* with its classical composition. Marthe's melancholy mood, the unaccustomed *chic* of her black fur, the sadness of her look beneath her winter hat are expressed with a special kind of elegance, dramatic and tender at the same time. This portrait has been allotted to different dates by different writers; perhaps because Bonnard, without altering it radically, went back to it more often than any other.

At the Petit-Palais is a picture which gives an idea of what Bonnard looked like when he was working. It is a portrait by Vuillard showing him at home on the Boulevard des Batignolles, 'brush in one hand, rag in the other' in a room furnished with a table, a sofa, a gilt-framed mirror and a little bronze by Maillol on the mantelpiece. The canvas is fixed to the wall by four drawing pins. To start his picture off, Bonnard has drawn a few lines in charcoal. Then, still standing, he has started to paint in little touches, his nose almost touching the canvas. He steps

back, stops, moves forward again, rubs a touch of colour with his finger to damp down its brilliance. While Bonnard watches the wall, Pouce, the excitable little dog, watches its master. Perhaps he will open the door at last, and they will both go out.

A house-painter had once said to Bonnard, 'Painting the first coat is always all right. I want to see the second.'

He never attempted the second coat too early.

He left the work on one side and came back to it later with a clearer eye. And weeks later, he would come back to it again; even after years had passed, he might still change a detail.

In one collector's flat, he asked in the pantry for a stool so that he could add some essential half-tones to the foliage in a picture which had

Le Basset, pencil drawing

BASKET OF FRUIT, 1928-1930

been hanging there for years. In the gallery of his friend Jacques Rodrigues he took down some drawings ('They aren't nailed to the wall, are they?'), had the glass taken off, and made an imperceptible correction with a rubber.

Visiting the Musée du Luxembourg one day, he went up to one of the pictures, took from his pocket a tiny box of paints and a brush the size of a toothpick, and added to one of the consecrated canvases a few minute touches that set his mind at rest. Meanwhile Vuillard tried to distract the attendant.

How is it possible to date works that are constantly added to and finished only when the painter says 'I can't see what more I could do to it?'

He almost always hesitated for a long time before signing a canvas, but sometimes, unexpectedly, he would declare, 'I'll readily sign that.' Bonnard did not paint from life, but his pockets were full of sketches made to assist his memory. He scrawled them with 'a burnt match, even a broken pen,' as George Besson tells us. 'But he had a predilection for an indescribable blunt pencil which was so short that a landscape or a nude seemed to spring from the ends of his three fingers compressed round an invisible point.'

Campagne (now known as *Pastorale*), *Town Landscape, Monuments, Paradise*—these are the four decorative compositions, shown in his 1921 Bernheim-Jeune exhibition, that give us the measure of the trial that Bonnard passed through between 1915 and 1919, the years in which he

THE BATHTUB, 1935

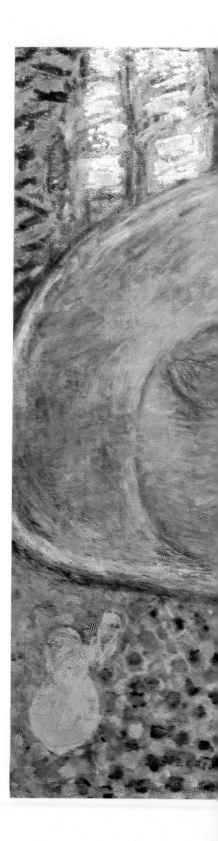

chained himself to the worst of the difficulties that faced him—it is wonderful to feel this happening in his work—and freed himself of them for ever.

great square grey house at about the same time. The lovely garden and its patio reminded Bonnard of the chestnut-trees at Villeneuve and Le Grand-Lemps.

Sketch for The Rape of Europa, pencil drawing

As a relaxation from his technical exercises, he painted *L'Estérel*, which led to the *Rape of Europa* with its waves breaking on white rocks.

At the end of the war, Bonnard went to Oullins, near Lyons, where my Uncle Thadée (to my mother's horror) had taken over the running of a munition factory. We came to stay at the

Thadée had not had much time to beautify this charmless structure, with its depressing furniture and its dark curtains. The few pretty objects that had been added rather emphasized than relieved its austere ugliness. And yet it was there that Bonnard started his portrait of Reine, Thadée's second wife. To do so he came back

Landscape, pen and wash drawing

126   *Sketch for Nude Crouching in Bathtub, pencil drawing*

NUDE CROUCHING IN BATHTUB, 1935

to Oullins with his dog Ubu, of course, and with Marthe, who fell seriously ill. One morning, my uncle, who had got up very early, was surprised to find him downstairs, unshaven, his bare feet thrust into old slippers, his eyes lost behind his spectacles, gazing through a french window at the dawn. This moment of anguish was one of the rare occasions when Bonnard's feelings overcame his habitual reserve.

Fortunately, Marthe recovered once more. Bonnard's little notebook filled with the sinuosities of the Saône. The *Portrait of Reine Natanson* —now in the Musée d'Art Moderne—was finished in 1921. It shows a young woman in a clear bluish-pink light, wearing a light *déshabillé*. She is like a doe; Reine had the eyes of a doe, but no more.

Bonnard's nuances of colour mask the ungrateful décor that Vuillard would perhaps have depicted in minute detail. Vuillard, with a master's touch, disentangled the telephone wires of Anna de Noailles, and the fringes of her oriental shawls, filtered the light of the electric lamp over the Louis XVI bed, polished the smallest knick-knack of the interiors he painted after the war. Bonnard told him this was all 'jewellery'.

In the south of France Bonnard often visited Renoir, who once said to him 'Always beautify'.

Many years later, Bonnard explained this to Angèle Lamotte. 'Renoir was above all a painter of Renoirs. He often had models whose skin was dull and grey, and he painted them like mother-of-pearl.'

128

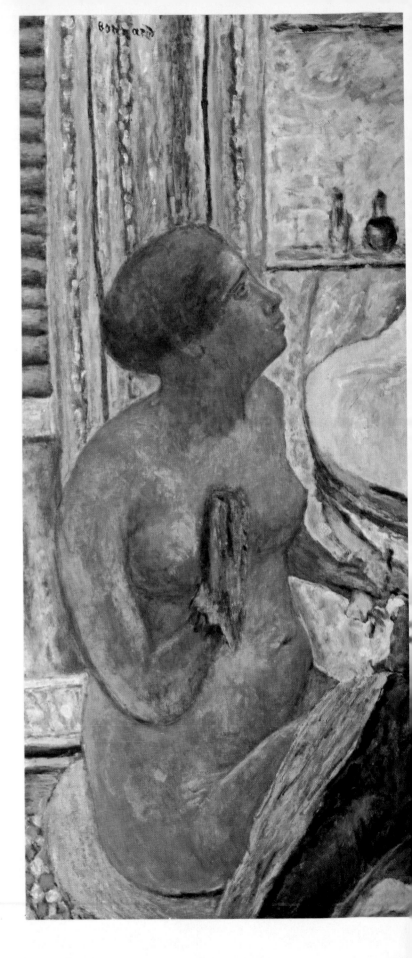

NUDE WITH HORSEHAIR
GLOVE, 1939

NUDE IN BATHTUB, 1935

129

In 1919, the year of Renoir's death, Bonnard painted *L'Ile heureuse*, a dappled gem in the middle of the Seine, delicate as a *fête galante*, almost too harmonious, a dream. Twenty-six years later when he visited his old friend Thadée and saw this seductive little oval picture, he took it in his hands, smiled, and said simply, 'Painters must lie.'

'To lie' may mean 'to choose from what is true and to add to the truth'—in other words, 'always beautify'.

L'Ile heureuse is in the Musée d'Art Moderne, hung above a door; it is hard to see.

Bonnard admired Titian and the eighteenth century, Cézanne, Degas, Monet, Renoir and Seurat. Rouault and Picasso interested him. He loved Matisse, who was so different from him in everything and who played a greater part in his life when Vuillard was dead and Marthe no longer there.

Some pictures by Laprade provoked from Bonnard the remark that 'They prove that it is possible for a painter who has charm to acquire power, but never the other way round.'

Picasso rejects Bonnard's sensitivity.

In 1920 the Bonnards stayed for a while at Arcachon. The wet sands at low tide under the swell of the clouds, the different quality of the sky, initiated Bonnard to the light of the Atlantic.

In 1921, after a journey in Rome where he visited the art galleries—he never stayed in them long, as he never stayed long in front of his model—he painted the *Piazza del Popolo* with a fruit-seller in transposed colours.

On Sundays, in the Arcadian setting of L'Etang-la-Ville, Roussel, an Aegipan in corduroy or raw wool, would receive his friends under the trees. Flanked by his 'Palotins'—the dogs of the Ubu dynasty—Bonnard sometimes came with Marthe in his sit-up-and-beg Ford landaulet, 8023 E 4. In her raglan coat and hat with a cord hanging from it, Marthe had created a *style Poiret* all her own. She no longer wanted to learn to drive. 'There's nothing to do any more, it just goes of its own accord...'

Nevertheless, Bonnard always had to open the bonnet and at least change one of 8023 E 4's sparking-plugs before they could set off again. In the photograph the car seems as ancient today as the little Zèbre with brass lamps in which he had trundled through Norman lanes, sketch-books in his pockets, to visit my parents at Villerville in 1908.

Still at the beginning of the twenties, just after my marriage, Pierre Charbonnier and I were passing through Saint-Tropez one winter day and stopped at L'Oustalet, the house where Manguin later lived, to say hello to the Bonnards. L'Oustalet was a modern house like a little fortress, squeezed between the road and the sea which seemed to come in through the great windows. We had a very friendly welcome and they invited us to stay to dinner, but beforehand we went down to the town with Bonnard who had been despatched to buy some food. A freezing Mistral was shaking the masts of the fishing boats. My most vivid memory is of the woman at the grocer's cutting slices of ham two fingers

THE JETTY, *c.*1934

thick under the abstracted gaze of Bonnard. At L'Oustalet, during the meal, two plates had been placed on the ground on either side of the great fireplace for the excited pair of dachshunds. Each bolted its share with incredible speed before darting across to attack the already empty plate of the other.

Marthe had started to draw. I can remember a bold charcoal drawing of a sort of branch representing a pine, and a pastel of a very orange orange with its little green leaf. In Paris, in the airy, neat, sparsely furnished flat in the Rue Mo-

Illustration for La 628-E 8

litor where they spent short periods between the south of France and La Roulotte, Louise Hervieu initiated Marthe into painting.

Herself a sick woman with a wild sensitivity that shone through the deep blacks and flaky greys and whites of her wonderful illustrations for rare books, Louise Hervieu was a forceful apparition in a hat, with a gift for lyrical but sincere flattery. She attributed Marthe's unbalance to her health, and perhaps she was not

entirely wrong. To distract Marthe from her bad dreams, Louise, who knew how to talk to sick children, patiently tried to teach her to draw.

On big white sheets of paper laid on the floor, she started by teaching Marthe to draw sticks. 'When you can do that, we will go on to something else.'

Bonnard, who perhaps regretted never having had a master himself, was fascinated. 'It wouldn't be a bad idea if you gave me some lessons.' He amused Louise considerably. She herself was very weak in health, always between two relapses, never at a loss for an epic tale of martyrdom in a hospital bed. She had braved the disapproval of a highly respectable family—one of her uncles was an Academician and author of a history of the crusades—to have a breathless affair with Fénéon. I do not think she ever had another.

Pierre did not need to draw sticks : but as he cut his pieces of canvas, by guesswork, to a size which would allow him to expand the sky of his picture as much as he liked, the contrast between his freedom and the rigidity of Louise was striking. Marthe was made to consider her model —even if it were only an apple—in relation to the surface against which she was to draw it. This gave him food for thought. He raised his eyebrows in astonishment when he heard Louise tell her pupil : 'Take a piece of paper and *box in* your subject.'

It was at this period that Bonnard went to see the hanging of an exhibition of works by Roussel's son-in-law Jacques Salomon at the Galerie Druet. He cordially invited Salomon to

THE JETTY, 1938-1939

133

come and stay at L'Oustalet after the exhibition closed with his young wife, Annette, whom Pierre and Marthe had known all her life. Vuillard smiled sceptically. He knew Marthe's moods and her neurotic crises only too well; he was one of the very few people who knew how to handle her.

In the afternoon, at the *vernissage*, Annette and Jacques saw a shamefaced Bonnard arrive. 'Of course we shan't discuss anything connected with painting. Each will work independently.' The young couple understood. Marthe had decided they were undesirable.

A few months later, Annette Salomon nevertheless paid her customary visit to Marthe when the Bonnards were in Paris. There was a frightful scene which reduced the younger woman to tears. Marthe had shouted 'Your husband wanted to watch Pierre working, he wanted to steal all his tricks...'

Her poor suspicious mind was assailed by fears which drove away even her most faithful friends, even, last of all, Louise. At the end of her life Marthe could hardly bear herself any more. Pierre always refused to leave her or to allow her to be moved or looked after by others. But there were still many good days and happy times. Marthe would take her parasol and, in a cotton dress and white canvas shoes with heels, she would go down towards the Seine with Pierre and he would part the high grass for her.

His sleeves rolled up, he would row with all the strength of his thin arms, then let the boat drift down past the islands. He loved to do this, as he loved his brisk early morning walks, with head bowed, through the fields.

Sometimes a large car would stop outside La Roulotte, and Monet, a portly patriarch in a flowing beard and a vast straw hat, would descend from it with his daughter-in-law Blanche to inspect Bonnard's latest pictures. He never commented on them, but a smile from this taciturn old man was enough for Bonnard.

On the inconvenient, charming wash-stand, next to the basin, Pierre placed a white vase decorated with cherries that he won at the fair at Vernon. Each summer he filled it with wild flowers, poppies whose one day of beauty he fixed for eternity. Monet loved the gaiety of these simple bouquets.

Pierre and Marthe also used to go to lunch at Giverny, minus the dogs which Monet detested because they made a noise and spoilt the borders in his magnificent garden. Pierre and Marthe would come back dazzled by irises and water-flowers. Later, his naked young women in bathtubs were perhaps to bear a dreamlike resemblance to Monet's wistarias against a blue sky.

Bonnard considered that painters should look more often at chromolithographs. One can see what he meant: the intoxicated sunsets, the Riviera landscape in delirium.

'The colour that so excites you' was now once more completely in Bonnard's power. He was to remain its master for ever. *The Harbour at*

Cannes, that staggering apotheosis of sunset, and *Signac Sailing* on an improbable azure sea, are the astonishing prelude to his greatest fanfares of colour.

Bonnard painted his own portrait in the mirror at this period: he has shaven off his beard, a dentist has filed down his projecting incisors, and great round spectacles have replaced the little steel-rimmed pince-nez.

Vuillard used to come to Vernonet with the Hessels in their Hispano-Suiza. Jos Hessel—a Belgian journalist who had been attracted to Paris by *La Revue Blanche*—began his business career with the Bernheim-Jeune brothers on the Avenue de l'Opéra where their gallery had moved after leaving the Rue Laffitte (they later transferred to the Boulevard de la Madeleine). Hessel was an inveterate gambler although his luck at

Illustration for La 628-E 8

poker sometimes deserted him; he turned his attention to painting as soon as he arrived. His flat in the Rue de Naples became a treasure-house of Cézannes, Redons, Maillols, Renoirs... The opulent dining-room contained Bonnard's picture of the dog Ubu hanging round a table and his large painting of Marthe, under the chestnut-trees, eating *The Cherry Tart*.

His scarlet portrait of Jos Hessel shows a rather frightening sort of vulture. Vuillard outlined him with less violence, hinting at the softness of his fat, beringed hand as it shook ash from his habitual cigar. So Jos Hessel looked when, lost in dreams of gold, he sat in the depths of his armchair in the shop in the Rue La Boétie, ready to welcome some superior client with a maxim from his repertoire or some really outrageous remark at which he would laugh himself.

The large panel by Bonnard, so delicate in its harmonies, which shows young girls in a boat on the surface of a pond with ducks and water-chestnuts floating on it, and which is now in the Musée d'Art Moderne, served for a long time to conceal from view the secret treasures of the back room in the Rue La Boétie.

Hessel was devious (his less skilful rivals used to use the phrase 'to lie like Hessel') but generous. He yielded without protest to the costly charities of his wife, who had a heart of pure gold.

Lucy Hessel was a tall, bony woman whose outlines time mysteriously seemed to soften. Bonnard liked her, in spite of the liaison between her and Vuillard which lasted forty years

SELF-PORTRAIT, 1939-1942

137

and brought Vuillard into contact with a world
that was not his own. After certain social occasions that were forced on him by his situation,
Vuillard would say to his closest friends 'Silence
guards me,' and would go back with ever-
increasing delight to his re-creation of the fluffy
textures of his mother's old cotton dressing-
gowns.

Pierre and Marthe were extremely particular
about hygiene, especially with regard to the
choice and preparation of food; but Ma Campagne, an anglers' inn at Vernon, met with their
approval and they often used to eat there. This
was where they put up their occasional guests.
In this inn, with its clandestine couples climbing
the stairs after lunch to take their siestas, Reine
and Thadée Natanson spent many holidays.
Bonnard was very attached to Thadée, who re-
vered him in return. Between Reine and Marthe
there grew up an uneasy sort of friendship whose
amiable appearances have been recorded by
Bonnard. In more than one of his pictures Reine
appears beside Marthe who wears the astonishing
red-striped creation that reflected her high spirits
at summer meals in the open air at Ma Campagne or on the terrace of Ma Roulotte.

For thirty years it did not occur to the 'Bonnards' to regularize their union, but one day
Marthe was upset by hearing some foolish woman refer to another as 'one of those women
men don't marry'. The next day Pierre took the
necessary steps and a marriage was arranged.

Pierre was too much aware of femininity not
to have been attracted by other faces and other

Illustration for Histoires naturelles

138

THE TERRACES, 1941

bodies, but, however pleasant his affairs might be, as soon as he felt that Marthe suspected something, he put a stop to the affair by retreat and silence. This sometimes led to unhappiness and dramatic scenes. The secretive Pierre, touched by remorse, would confess to Thadée or another close friend: 'You see, I haven't much courage...'

Marthe's ideas of personal adornment never rose any higher than cheap finery. In furniture, a mixture of pitch-pine, wickerwork, and folding canvas chairs satisfied a shared taste for eccentric discomfort; but she always felt the need to lather herself, scrub herself, and massage herself with a sort of meticulous sensuousness, for hours on end. When she finally achieved the only luxury she had ever longed for, a real bathroom with running water, Pierre found a way—as he had with the galvanized tub, the jug and the little wooden towel rail—to transform the pipework, the new tiles, the little white stool, the aggressive ceramic fitments, into an opalescent setting for a fairy-tale.

The same miracle takes place when he transforms a table with various articles on it—a brown coffee-pot, a saucepan that has been left on the tablecloth, a half-empty dish, a bread-basket, the fruits of the earth—into the blend of the humble and the exquisite which fills his succulent still-lifes.

During the twenties Bonnard illustrated Mirbeau's *Dingo* and Vollard's *La Vie de Sainte-Monique*. On a short visit to the United States in 1926 to act as a member of the jury for the

Sainte Monique, pen drawing

VIEW OF ROOFS AT LE CANNET, 1941-1942

141

Carnegie prize, he visited many public and private collections. In the house of one Washington collector he asked for a brush and some paint to retouch one of his pictures.

Paris retained first place in his heart, although he no longer spent more than two months there each year. It was at Le Cannet that he painted, from sketches, *Le Café du Petit Poucet*, a pendant to *La Place Clichy*.

'I am thinking about my decoration,' he wrote to the Bessons, 'and it is beginning to take shape in my mind. I hope you will have patience; these things have to mature—like an apple—and the process can't be speeded up.'

In the following year he completed his gay, joyful portrait of a little girl, Isabelle Lecomte de Nouy, playing with her dog on a bench.

When he carried this charming picture, wrapped up as usual in newspaper, to Mme Félix Vallotton, the child's grandmother, he countered the enthusiastic praise which greeted the picture with the words: 'Yes, there are some good things, but I have a lot to answer for.'

Pierre Courthion visited Bonnard in his studio in the Rue Tourlaque in 1932. 'He looked as though he felt the cold,' writes M. Courthion. 'He had greying, close-cropped hair, a scrawny neck, and eyes of gentle brilliance behind his glasses... dressed in dark colours.'

At the beginning of 1933 Bonnard was preparing for a spring exhibition that was to be put on by the Bernheims at the same time as a retrospective of his portraits at the Galerie Braun. He wrote to George Besson in February: 'I am making an effort to renew myself a little; *they* will just repeat what they were saying in 1900.'

He still moved moved between Paris, Vernon and Arcachon but after 1925 he spent most of his time at Le Cannet, above Cannes, where he had bought the last of his houses. Le Bosquet was a little villa of the type built by speculators on the Côte d'Azur for retired people. Its pink walls nestled against a slope planted with olives and dwarf apple-trees. In January the mimosa put on all its splendour and the persimmons produced their brilliantly coloured fruit. There were two fig-trees and a shivering pepper-plant. Artichokes were massed in chaotic profusion. The ground-floor room was all white—the door, the radiator, the fireplace—a brilliant setting for the convent chairs, the tiled floor, the open window. Upstairs the rooms were small and in the minute studio there was no room to step back from the canvas. As always there was one large piece of canvas fixed to the wall, on which Bonnard painted several pictures at once, separated by lines of white paint.

Before breakfast Bonnard would whistle for his dog and go on the daily walk which supplied the green oaks, the rocks, the tousled branches that he later set down at leisure. All that his windows revealed—the landscape, crowned with palm-trees and blotched with nasty factory-made tiles, that runs down to the incandescent sea—all this he flooded with colour, using its unreality to reveal its fundamental truth.

'Our God is light,' he said to a young artist, 'and one day you will understand what that means.'

142

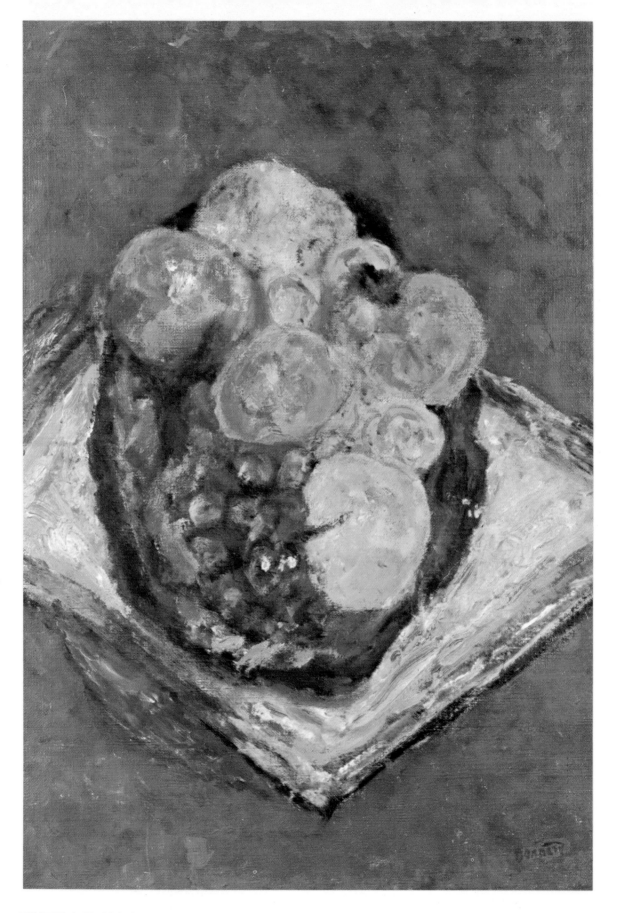

PEACHES AND GRAPES, 1943

'How beautiful! How young and fresh!' cried Jacques Rodrigues in front of a painting of Le Cannet.

'A bonbon from the South', was Bonnard's reply.

His real preference was for a different sky. 'The light of the North is more interesting than the southern sunlight because it is always changing... It was Boudin who introduced me to Deauville. He said there was no other place in France where the sky was so beautiful and so varied,' Bonnard told Ingrid Rydbeck, a Stockholm journalist sent to interview him in 1937.

Between 1932 and 1938 he made repeated visits to Deauville and Trouville. Indifferent to the ugliness of the flowered wallpaper on which he pinned his canvases, he worked in anonymous hotel-rooms to re-compose the light of the Norman seaboard, orchestrating it with a gleam of brass. Ochreous at first, his yellow tints kindle the clouds, the houses, the hulls of the fishing-boats. Bonnard became so fascinated by yellow, after the blue Riviera, that he later bathed a nude in yellow light. Even the still waters of the Gulf of Saint-Tropez he paints yellow as the sun, under round, peony-red clouds.

One day Jacques Rodrigues had said of a picture by Signac, 'There is a lot of yellow in it.'

'One can't have too much,' said Bonnard. Just before he died, when he was already too weak to hold the brush himself, it was a touch of yellow that he asked his nephew Charles to add to his last painting. 'On the left, at the bottom, there on the ground under the almond tree.'

'During the whole of my life I have seen the world gradually become suffused with light,' wrote Teilhard de Chardin, 'Everything round me now has an inner luminosity.' Pierre Bonnard could have said the same thing. His painting too is the result of Divine grace.

In 1936 Bonnard was awarded the second Carnegie prize; the first prize went to a certain Leon Kroll. Bonnard was too modest not to accept what John Rewald called 'this humiliating honour'. But nevertheless, in 1912, along with Vuillard, Roussel and Vallotton, he had refused the Légion d'Honneur.

In 1937 Vuillard bowed to affectionate pressure from Maurice Denis, Georges Desvallières and David Weill, and, partly to avoid disappointing Lucy Hessel, he allowed his name to go forward as a candidate for the Académie des Beaux-Arts.

When Bonnard heard that his friend had been made an academician, he assumed his most impish air. 'Good!' he said. 'That will teach him!'

Bonnard was then working on the splendid *Nude in the Bath* that now hangs in the Petit-Palais. This work was a sort of wager with himself. 'I shall never dare to embark on such a difficult subject again. I still can't get the effect I want. I have been working on it for six months and it will take me several more months to finish it.'

He worked on this subject, on several canvas, over a period of two years; but his final triumph was absolute. Everything was speeding up, as it always does at the approach of a cata-

Garden in the South of France, pencil drawing
Overleaf: The Bay of Cannes from le Bosquet, pen drawing

147

LANDSCAPE ON THE COTE D'AZUR, 1943

clysm. 1937 was the year of the International Exhibition, and Bonnard's decorations for the Palais de Chaillot mark the highest point of his achievement. Nature in flower, a little bridge over the sparkling water, the ox and the ass, a naked child and some lambs on the blue grass —this is the Nativity of spring. When Sam Salz congratulated him, he held up his hands and said : 'The only chance I have ever had to work on a large surface, and I failed to make good use of it, as usual...'

That was Bonnard at the age of seventy.

Illustration for Les Histoires du Petit Renaud

THE OX AND THE CHILD, 1945

Illustration for Prométhée mal enchaîné

Nude Washing, four pencil drawings

153

155

SUNSET

Illustration for Marie

Once again war broke out. Bonnard did not leave Le Cannet until after the Liberation. Vuillard, sick at heart, broken by defeat, died in the confusion of the exodus. Bonnard never again allowed him to be mentioned in his presence. But in the decoration in honour of Saint François de Sales that he did in the Parish Church of Assy in Savoy in 1945, the portrait of the saint which appears in stained-glass blues, purples and mauves, above a grey, suffering human race, is not entirely inspired by contemporary prints. There is something in the roundness of the rosy head, the flame-like beard—an individual gravity—that recalls his beloved friend.

It was Dom Willibrod Verkade, the former *Nabi Obéliscal,* now a Benedictine monk, who said in his book *Le Tourment de Dieu* that Vuillard resembled François de Sales.

It was probably during the winter of 1940-1941 that Bonnard wrote to Besson: 'Our life here is rather solitary and as organized as it can be. Today is a bad day. It has been snowing since this morning. The daily help is ill. The electricity is not working and the milk will probably not come tonight. Apart from that, everything is quite in order...'

At this dark period a new note of rapture enters Bonnard's sun-drenched landscapes; they become hymns celebrating nature at its most joyous.

But it was cold and his hands were frozen. 'I saw Bonnard again in Cannes in 1941,' says Claude Dauphin. 'He was still painting his magnificent Provençal landscapes. He told me he had come down to see the mayor of Cannes to try and get a little coal, and he asked me if I could help. But at that time there was hardly enough coal to heat the gaming-room at the Casino, and I do not think he got any.'

Food was rationed, and paint, too, was becoming scarce. On 15 January, 1941 Bonnard wrote to George Besson: '... I hasten to reassure you about my coupons. The rest of my allocation has been allowed on the strength of my reputation as an honest citizen, but now I have my papers there aren't enough food supplies. There's a real famine this month, perhaps it will get better soon. I hope so for several reasons. Another thing that has been worrying me is the supply of paint. I have received supplies from many very kind friends, and I am now well stocked up. Thank you, my dear Besson, for having tried to save me from starving for want of coupons. But I am weathering the storm, as Signac would say.'

It was a far cry from the time when there was no difficulty in supplementing Marthe's diet with sardines mashed in cod-liver oil for her anaemia. While waiting for his tubes of paint to arrive, Bonnard turned to gouache and water-colour. From time to time, kind neighbours brought him—without any thought of a return—

an egg, a few extremely scarce potatoes, a little coffee, half a pound of black-market sugar. One morning they were amazed and overcome to see Bonnard's cleaning woman arrive bearing a great roll of water-colours tied up with an old bootlace. Bonnard, who always paid his debts, was minimizing his own 'going rate' at a time when speculation on his work was becoming more and more active.

'Bonnard is on the Côte d'Azur, not giving anybody much news of himself,' wrote Maurice Denis to Dom Verkade. 'His work is fetching very high prices and attracting the dealers to Le Cannet.'

Bonnard was an independent, a free man. Vuillard admired him as much for his essential wisdom as for his painting. The moment his pictures began to fetch prices which seemed unreasonable to him, he refused to sell them, not because he wanted to keep them, but because he considered that 'people were being robbed.' He yielded only when he needed a little money.

On 26 January, 1942 Marthe Bonnard died. No one ever entered her room again. Pierre locked the door on it, just as he did on his own secret grief. Vollard, Roussel, Fénéon, Maurice Denis also vanished from the scene.

Bonnard painted a large nude of Dina Vierny, dark, powerful, golden, proud, of a different breed from the nudes of the past. But after Marthe's death he asked someone to give a message to Louise Hervieu. 'Tell her how tired I am of it all.'

RED ROOFS AT LE CANNET, 1942

Meanwhile his landscapes seem woven from the silk of dreams, and his magic fruits are opalescent treasures fished from the deep.

Going down to market in Cannes with his shopping basket, very tall and thin in his voluminous overcoat, his espadrilles and his canvas hat, he looked less like an old man than a young man grown very old. And as he grew gradually more remote from physical life, his pictures too became disembodied, swamped in pure colour.

159

The Circus, pen drawing

One remembers the expression 'violent tachism' that Gustave Geffroy had used in 1892.

Visitors to Le Cannet had the feeling that they were in the way; he could be surly and unforthcoming. But then suddenly he would come out of his shell, pick a few roses, and become himself again; indulgent, delightful, and as dissatisfied with himself as ever. He said to a young painter, Jean Bazaine (who was never to forget it), 'I am just beginning to understand, and I ought to start all over again.'

Bonnard made two brief visits to Paris after the war, to see once again the Place Clichy, the Tuileries, the movement in the streets, and above all, his friends: Georges d'Espagnat, Thadée Natanson, George Besson, Misia—the few still alive.

He painted another *Self-Portrait*—worn, pale, his eyes dark and tormented—against the dead tiled background that had belonged to his lost girls in the bath.

This man with his face marked by suffering seems to be waiting for the great white horse that he finished painting while staying with his nephew at Fontainebleau before he went back to Le Cannet to die. Where did he see it, this *Circus Horse*? It is a runaway phantom—the horse on which the bareback rider of his youth had whirled—and its hoofbeat announces the last hour of his life.

Bonnard lay sick, his face to the wall; the joy of seeing was finished for him in this world. On 23 January 1947, before dawn, he closed his eyes and discovered the unimaginable shores of death.

LAST SELF-PORTRAIT, 1944-1945

161

162   *Etching for Sainte Monique*

A MEMOIR BY HANS R. HAHNLOSER
with notes by Mme Hedy Hahnloser-Bühler

In his preface to the catalogue of a commemorative exhibition at the Galerie Bernheim-Jeune in 1950, Charles Terrasse, Bonnard's favourite nephew, records these words of his uncle: 'My friends? Where are they? I have hardly any left.' But he still smiled with pleasure at the thought of seeing Georges d'Espagnat, Thadée Natanson, George Besson, Mme Hahnloser... and Henri Matisse. The link between our two families had started around 1910 when Félix Vallotton, who had painted a portrait of my mother in Winterthur two years earlier, introduced my parents to his friends the Nabis. It lasted, through letters and through personal contact, more than thirty years, until Bonnard's death.

Bonnard's great portrait of the Hahnloser family (*The Sea Trip*, see p. 105), the Nabi paintings that are to be found in many public and private collections in Winterthur, and many books and articles on the Nabis and their age, all bear witness to this connection.

In 1910, to declare oneself for the Nabis was an act of daring. And yet in 1916, in the new Museum of Fine Arts in Winterthur, there opened a large exhibition of contemporary French painting which included four Bonnards: the largest selection of his work to be shown

outside France before the 1928 New York exhibition. The catalogue includes an introduction by Théodore Duret, the first historian of the Impressionists, as well as the following notice: 'For prices apply to the cashier, the curator or M. R. Bühler, Dr Arthur Hahnloser or M. G. Reinhart.' No clearer indication could be found of the private character of this gallery, which was the creation of these three men and their families.

Robert Rittmeyer had designed for them a building whose lighting has remained a model to other architects; they ran it, and they arranged and hung the various exhibitions. The titular curator found himself reduced to an almost exclusively administrative role. Liaison with Paris was in the hands of a Winterthur painter, Charles Montag, who had the *entrée* to the principal galleries, Bernheim-Jeune, Druet, Durand-Ruel and Vollard.

My mother possessed an amazingly sure intuition which complemented my father's practical wisdom. At a time when he was still in practice as an oculist (my mother was his assistant at first) he gave a new impulse to the Winterthur Society of Friends of Art. Every Tuesday, at the so-called 'Café de la Villa Flora', once the home of my great-grandfather, meetings were held

163

which have left their mark on the artistic life of our city.

My parents had their habit of spending ten days in Paris twice a year in order to make the rounds of the studios and galleries. They generally met their friends at Roussel's house in L'Etang-la-Ville, although they sometimes visited Maillol at Marly-le-Roi or joined other guests of Henri Manguin. According to Jacques Salomon, Roussel's son-in-law, their annual visit was something of an event; their Parisian friends were eager to know what was thought of them abroad—and in Paris as well.

Bonnard used to meet them at the Café de la Régence, or in a *bistro* near his studio. After 1923, when my parents began to spend their winters in Cannes for the sake of my mother's health, they always set aside Thursday as 'Bonnard day'. On that day they would eat together at La Pauline, my parents' house by the sea, or perhaps go to Bonnard's studio. When one of the 'absent friends' turned up—Vallotton from Cagnes, Maillol from Banyuls or Matisse from Nice—they would all meet at La Croisette. Thanks to these close and constant contacts my parents were able to collect a number of masterpieces of painting, in addition to numerous drawings and prints.

Their best propaganda outlet was the 'Salle des Français' at the Winterthur Museum, where they would deposit their most recent acquisitions on loan. Their example was followed by a succession of other members of the Society of Friends of Art, so that today, quite apart from the large collections, there are many modern French paintings scattered in private houses in Winterthur.

A picture presented to the Winterthur Museum by the author of these lines and his sister possesses great historic interest : Vallotton's *The Five Painters* (c. 1902), an intimate pendant to Maurice Denis' *Tribute to Cézanne* (1901). Incidentally, Denis' painting does not include Vallotton, who was doubtless preoccupied at the time by his wedding. In the foreground Bonnard is the guiding spirit of the discussion; one can feel the exchange of ideas taking place between these friends who, unlike any other modern group of artists, stayed in touch with each other all their lives. As well as this key picture, the Museum has five Bonnards, four Vuillards, eight Vallottons, Roussel's great murals and two of the masterpieces of Maillol.

Bonnard, Vuillard, Roussel and Vallotton were the contemporaries of my parents. My mother's interest in their work stemmed also from the fact that she had contributed decorative work to the *Jugendstil* movement. Her cousin Richard Bühler was for a long time the president of the *Werkbund*. In my opinion, Bonnard's early works, even more than those of Vuillard and Vallotton, are the most extreme examples of *Jugendstil*. It was this same *Jugendstil* that first gave pride of place to abstract stylistic elements. The polyptych on page 29, for example, leaves one wondering whether it was the theme that determined the form or the other way round. This is the first appearance, in our age, of form treated entirely in its own right, the first of a series of experiments that were to be pursued by Cubism, Constructivism and Tachism.

From his very earliest works Bonnard combines very clear sense of structure with a predilection for tall, narrow formats. The influence of Japanese prints? Certainly, but even more it was the adaptation of the surface to the artist's personality. All his life he was looking for 'built pictures'. Later he frequently introduced this kind of framework into the pictures themselves. The scene is limited by pillars, or seen through a door or a window; and it often has a horizontal basis consisting of a table or a mantelpiece. Later still, the structure of his paintings, reduced to vibrant bands of colour, came close to abstraction and became once more what it had been in his first works, a decorative element in which the subject of the picture is entirely submerged.

Another aspect of Bonnard's anticlassicism: his preference for the square format, which is detested by many painters because it deprives them of the advantages of the golden section inherent in standardized picture-formats. This neutral square surface Bonnard brings to life by throwing his composition off centre. 'To begin a picture,' he said to me one day, 'there must be an empty space in the centre.' And that is why he so often pushes the important objects in his pictures to the edge of the canvas, even when the object is his wife's head (p. 175). In *The Saucepans* he actually leaves this particular object out: Marthe's orange corsage is only there for the colour. These innovations are not the caprices of an eccentric out for originality at any price but a source of enrichment. They force us to think more carefully about what the artist's real intentions are.

This principle too, goes back to the debates of the Nabis. At their monthly meetings at l'Os à Moelle everyone present was expected to contribute an idea or a discovery, which might be a sketch, a poem or a model. Thus they acted as a force for progress which enriched the whole domain of painting, which in those days was almost exclusively orientated towards the outside world. 'The Impressionists have their ceiling too low', said Redon, the leader of the Symbolist quest for a new mysticism. The secret, the mysterious, the fanciful aspects of Bonnard the 'enchanter' lie at the root of all his magic. Every time, or almost every time, that I have tried to describe a Bonnard painting I have known for years, I have discovered something new in it; the upper part of Marthe's body (p. 108) or the basket-work chair hidden by the cloth in *Nude with Coverlet* (p. 65).

In her long work on *Félix Vallotton et ses amis*, published in 1935, Mme Hedy Hahnloser-Bühler pays tribute to the Swiss painter on whose behalf she had fought for so long, and gives pen-portraits of his friends the Nabis. Bonnard was the first to read this book in proof, and my mother's notes include this passage:

'Bonnard has just brought me the proofs. He was clearly deeply moved by what he had read. He had stayed up for two nights in order to finish it. "It is really us" he said, "and yet it is all so far away that it seems, reading about it, that it all happened to someone else. I would never have believed you capable of such a solid and sustained piece of work. It reads like a novel." His only suggested correction concerns a historical error : I had referred to Lautrec as the creator of the modern poster but this title really belongs to Bonnard himself. His poster for *France-Champagne* so delighted Toulouse-Lautrec that he asked Bonnard to take him to see the printer Ancourt so that he could learn about this new technique. Soon afterwards, with his customary élan, Lautrec produced a whole succession of large posters in the same vein. As soon as Bonnard saw them he decided

to leave Lautrec in possession of a field in which he had already surpassed him. Another proof of his critical sense, his modesty and his generosity.'

Bonnard's personality is described with great insight by Mme Vaillant in the present volume. Jean Cassou and Raymond Cogniat, for their part, examine the general problems raised by his art. I have therefore done no more than add my personal commentaries to some of the works reproduced. I have used the notes and memoirs my mother wrote for the benefit of the family and have tried to supplement them with stylistic analyses. These are not nearly frequent enough in the books that have been written about Bonnard.

Ice-Rink, 1897-1898

168   Fiacre, c.1895   Woman and Children, c.1894

Red Garters, c.1906

The Family of Claude Terrasse,
1908-1909

169

The Red Check Tablecloth, 1910-1911

The Haystack, 1915-1916

of Saint-Tropez, 1909-1910

The Seine at Vernon, 1911

annet from La Maison Rose, 1926

Garden near Toulon, 1915

Small Nude Leaning Forward, c.1918

The White Dress, 1912

Woman undoing her Chemise, c.1910

Red Garters, c.1906

Nude by Lamplight, c.1912

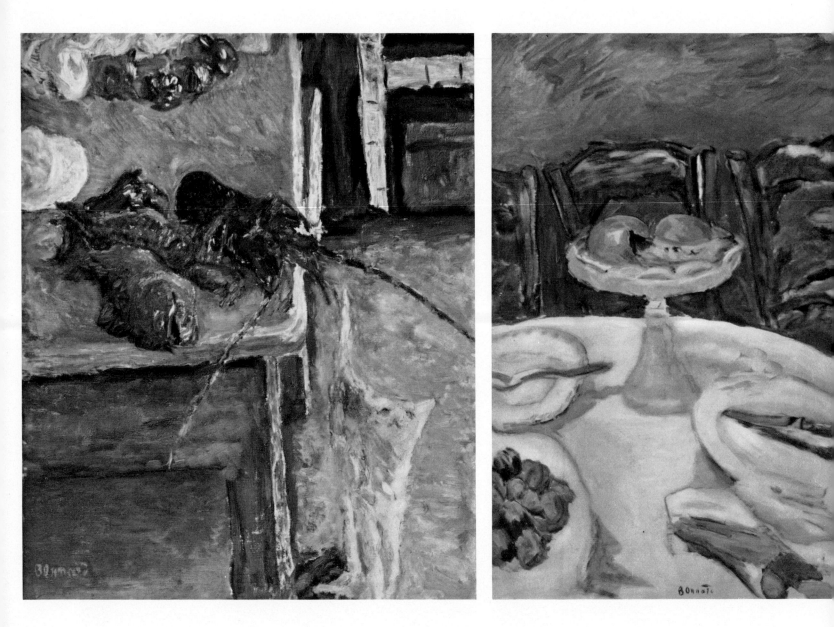

Bouillabaisse, c.1910   Fruit-dish with Oranges, 1912

able-napkins, c.1908

ill-life with Figure, 1912

Interior with the dog, Flac, 1912

176   Flowers from the South, 1914   Still-life with Apples, 1924

Peaches and Grapes by Lamplight,
1919

Sweet Peas, c.1910-1912

178   The Sea Trip, 1924. First version in blue and white

Hahnloser and her Skye Terrier,

Arthur Hahnloser, 1924
ches for *The Sea Trip*

ght, before 1914

Stormy Landscape, c.1909

180

Still-life with Plum-stones, 1932

NUDE WITH TOQUE AND NUDE WITH COVERLET 1911 (p. 65)

These two pictures bear the numbers 885 and 886 in the catalogue of Bonnard's work; this means that they date from 1911. They are two variants of the same idea. The first nude, seen from directly in front, is 'taken by surprise'; the second is more intimate, as if the artist had seen his model without being seen himself.

The first came to us direct from the Galerie Bernheim-Jeune and the second ten years later, from a German collection. Their elongated format recalls the eighteen-nineties and the 'decorative panels' that the Nabis painted under the influence of Japanese prints. 'No more easel paintings' was their motto. Bonnard remained faithful to this principle for longer than the others, and went further in its application of it. Not for nothing did his friends give him the title of '*Nabi japonard*', an epithet which he freely accepted. Apart from his first tall, thin paintings, he produced some five-colour lithographs that could be mounted on a screen *à la mode*; they depict four intersecting street scenes. One of these screens he later heightened with touches of gouache and framed. [1]

Women and Children (p. 168) dates from the same period, and the little boy is wearing the same fur hat. Bonnard had offered to paint this so that the child's parents should have a work to represent this period in their collection; but his modesty led him to content himself with the smallest study possible.

During the war, when my mother wrote the letter to Bonnard which is mentioned on page 182, I asked her to include a question as to his affinities with the Japanese. His answer is charming and a little paradoxical: he mentions the 'gaudiness of colour,' but not the compositional principles that so clearly influenced his work. No doubt this is because the idea of adapting the format of his canvases to suit his conception of the picture had become a basic principle of his art.

My mother writes of these two paintings: *On seeing this scene with its vibrant pink embodying all the radiance of Bonnard's art, a Parisienne who knew how simple a life he led exclaimed: 'How odd to think of poor Marthe in such an elegant hotel, with a bathroom.' This is not the right explanation for this scene of enchantment: the light gives it all its elegance. Bonnard never spent money on luxuries, it is true; but he also never confused luxury and comfort. To him the bathroom was a necessity and an inspiration. It is Bonnard's art that has created this amazing blue apartment out of a modest hotel-room with a place to wash in one corner behind a lacquered door. And the sumptuous, many-hued, silken coverlet, what humble couch does it conceal? Closer examination reveals that a white sheet has simply been draped over the arms of a perfectly ordinary basket-*

[1] According to Claude Roger-Marx, *Bonnard Lithographe*, Monte-Carlo, 1952, No. 47, this screen (150 cm x 200 cm) was published by Molines in 1899: but the fashion belongs to 1894, and J. T. Soby, J. Elliott and M. Wheeler, in *Bonnard and his Environment*, The Museum of Modern Art, New York, 1965, p. 51, allot the dates 1892-1894 to the copy with touches of gouache which is now in a private collection in New York.

work chair; it is just possible to detect the back of the chair with its adjustable bamboo supports. Bonnard's 'mystery of white' plays on a blue wall as if the light of the sky had entered into the blue of the room: just as the immaterial blue of Cézanne's skies becomes one with the landscape beneath. Bonnard has once more found a spiritual interpretation of everyday reality. He has turned 'nothing'—a simple room—into a miracle: this is the achievement of a poet.

I have to confess that although we saw this picture, and savoured the miraculous whiteness of the bed, every day for years, it is only now, reading these lines written by my mother, that we have discovered the humble basketwork chair concealed under the sheet. This illustrates two essential characteristics of Bonnard's art: whereas the Impressionists present us with an obvious reality, a Bonnard picture always has its secret, which may remain a secret until many years have passed; and he loves to find a place for some cloudy and indistinct shape—here the coverlet or the pink toque and what is beside it—which will allow the imagination to soar above mere concrete reality.

TEA, 1916 (p. 85) AND A LETTER FROM PIERRE BONNARD

Admired as his works are today, at the time many of them seemed hard to understand and hard to accept. His unexpected colours, above all, disturbed (and sometimes shocked) those who had come to know his work during his classical period shortly before the First War; this period is particularly well-represented in our collection. So members of our family were often to be heard saying: 'This year he has really gone too far, it is quite impossible to follow him.' But Bonnard was not deflected from his course—his last works, painted at the age of nearly eighty, include several which still seem puzzling to us today. *Tea*, painted in 1916, is one of the curious works I spoke of just now: even Bonnard, in the letter quoted below, speaks of a hat in the picture as 'outrageously blue'. The subject and the setting in themselves are a puzzle: when was Bonnard ever in such a palatial house? It cannot belong to friends; his personal belongings are there, his blue cigarette box and his white vase, and his wife Marthe is pouring the tea. Bonnard always abhorred the 'anecdote'; what he paints is not a 'scene' but has no interest except as a subject for a picture. Here Marthe dominates; she alone is active, she alone is studied, right down to the make-up she used in an attempt to restore her youth. The other women are merely guests: on her left, a face that is charming but only hinted at, then a very pretty but lifeless girl. On the extreme right is one of those cut-off profiles of which Bonnard was so fond. Only the woman's back in the foreground, with its strident colours, provides the sharp accent that Bonnard was to put into all his later pictures. Outside the window, the dark mass of the trees answers her black hair and contrasts with the pale yellow of the branches and the sky. In 1946, four years after this picture had been left to us by my father's brother, we were still arguing about it. So we asked our mother to ask Bonnard how such strange contrasts had come into being; and perhaps we hoped a little that he would alter the picture as he had altered *The Sea-Trip* in 1925 (p. 105)—of his own accord, naturally. Today our question may seem presumptuous : at least it illustrates the perplexity that his constant innovations caused even to his friends. His answer proves that the shock effect was conscious and intentional.

Villa du Bosquet, Le Cannet,
Alpes-Maritimes
(4 January, 1946)

Dear Mme Hahnloser,

I am glad to hear you are at Castagnola : a more temperate part of the world, I take it, than Winterthur. At the same time as your letter I received a Swiss Christmas number which showed you surrounded by your pictures and, I was glad to see, quite unchanged. I received a food-parcel from Switzerland a short time ago and am very touched by your concern for us. In the photograph I can see, by your feet, the picture you describe in your letter. I remember the hat, outrageously blue but quite truthful. This reminds me of the Japanese influence of which you speak. In my youth I was excited by the magnificent gaudiness of Japanese crepon—a sort of wove paper, used for popular art. Much later I learned to appreciate the beauty of the great Japanese engravers, who are soberer and reveal less about pure colour combinations. Fénéon called me *Bonnard très japonard*. Claude Monet is said to have discovered Japanese art in a grocer's shop in Holland when his purchase was wrapped in some prints, just as furniture used to be sold in Normandy wrapped in old tapestries.

I hope your stay in Castagnola is a happy one, and remain your devoted friend

P. Bonnard

THE SEA TRIP (THE HAHNLOSER FAMILY)
IN ITS VARIOUS STAGES, 1924-1925 (p. 105)

Mme Hahnloser writes : *Arthur several times asked his intimate friend Bonnard to paint a picture including one or more of us. 'I should like nothing better,' answered Bonnard. 'Give me the enchanted setting for a picture and I will do it ! One afternoon when we were going back to the islands with a good wind blowing, I appeared wearing an old pale blue jersey. 'That's it,' cried Bonnard, 'the enchantment that makes a painting.' The purity of 'Bonnard blue' had so caught his imagination that he settled down at the other end of the boat, drew out his sketchbook and started to draw. We told him that we could spend about 5,000 francs on the picture, and the very next day it was* *already roughed out on a canvas approximately 66 × 70 cm. Mme Bonnard, 'Marthe the demon' who was already beginning to suffer from mental disturbance, came on the scene. 'My dear Pierre,' she cried, 'why don't you go on and make it smaller ? You'll never get everything you want to say about the Hahnlosers on that little bit of canvas !' Bonnard said nothing, but the following Thursday (Thursday was the day when we used to go up to their house) the canvas on the wall was about twice as large. We were trying to explain, in our embarrassment, that we could not accept such a large picture, when Bonnard said calmly : 'All right, the rest will be a present for the Doctor, and there's and end to it.'*

In the first version 'Le père Arthur' has his back to the women and is gazing into the distance. 'A true sailor,' Bonnard explained, 'always looks at the horizon for a quarter of an hour before he sails. Your husband is a true sailor, isn't he ?'

It was clear that he had set out to make him the principal figure in the painting ; he was really fond of my husband.

Back in Paris, he wrote to us : 'I beg you to send me back the big canvas. Seldom have I bungled anything so completely. All one sees is the white of the sail.' This was a typical example of his conscientiousness. The picture came back to us a few months later with more life and more colour ; it seemed to have become the antithesis of what it had been. Vuillard and Vallotton, who were there to celebrate the occasion, explained that the picture had been improved because one could now see the volume of the figures. As for Bonnard, in the midst of the general rejoicing, he asked those present to estimate how much he had changed the size of the sail. This seemed easy, but the estimates reflected individual temperament very closely. Vuillard 'the just' kept close to a happy medium ; Vallotton the mathematician, came within an inch or so of the truth. The lady of the house was induced to guess as much as seventeen centimetres. Then, with an ironic smile, Bonnard told us. 'Not one centimetre,' he said. 'The illusion that the sail shrank enormously comes entirely from the heightening of the intensity of the colour, especially the blue of the sea. The effect of colour alters the proportions completely. This was a surprise and a lesson to me.'

Bonnard never made any sketches in colour ; the most he did was to make notes indicating the intensity of colour in figures, such as 'cobalt 20, blue 2, ochre 10'. A few detail drawings were all he needed to achieve a likeness in a portrait.

We illustrate several surviving sketches for *The Sea Trip* as well as the picture itself. These show clearly how the first version in oils sprang from the drawings, and the study of my mother is extremely alive; only the profile of my sister seems influenced by Bonnard's favourite feminine type.

'The presence of the object disturbs the artist,' Bonnard said one day. His work was done in the studio, away from his models, and is based on an inner vision which springs from the 'idea' he had of his picture. The first rough version in oils (p. 178) still looks like three juxtaposed portrait studies. The little pen-drawing, done in his studio (p. 104) shows him in search of a new composition : he detaches the figures from their background, giving the elements of the composition

—the sea, the boat, the sail—more space and more unity, and marks off the rectangle. Later still he settled on a square format—a difficult one even for him. It was only after eighteen months that he achieved the right tonality; a friendship of long-standing had given rise to a masterpiece.

THE JETTY, 1926-1934 (p. 131)
AND THE HAHNLOSER FAMILY'S PRIVATE VIEW

From about 1923 onwards Bonnard and my parents spent their winters at Cannes. Every year, he would invite us to his studio to show us the winter's 'harvest' of pictures. When this event coincided with my vacation (I was a student at Vienna and later assistant to Julius von Schlosser) I was allowed to be present. First one had tea—from a very old and odd assortment of cups and saucers—and then one went up to his tiny studio which had canvases pinned all over its walls. In his book *Le Bonnard que je propose*, his friend Thadée Natanson tells of a similar 'private view' Bonnard had given him in his Paris studio. Bonnard had the habit of painting on simple pieces of canvas, to avoid dependence on the standardized format imposed by ready-made 'stretchers', and to enable him to adapt his pictures as he thought fit. He often cut a strip from a canvas, or added one on. At the top of a large decorative panel entitled *Twilight* (p. 179) there is a strip of canvas three centimetres wide, while the painting extends round the sides of the stretcher. Here is my mother's account of the memorable occasion that Bonnard used to call 'the Hahnloser family's private view.'

Every spring, when Bonnard was collecting together the works for his annual exhibition, we were allowed a preview : we could study everything at leisure and tell him which pictures we wanted for our collection. For him this was a chance to talk about his work, and there is not one of his canvases in our collection whose choice he did not approve. He was glad to know that it would be possible to follow his entire evolution at Winterthur. Nothing illustrates this better than the history of the small picture entitled 'The Jetty' (p. 131). He began it in 1926 or 1928, but we had to wait at least seven years for it : he was always finding something he wanted to put right. Then one fine winter day in 1935, he said casually : 'If you still want to have 'The Jetty', it's ready. I have found out what was throwing it out of true. I have heightened this yellow effect ; everything is in balance now. It is small, but I think it is quite a successful piece of work.' These seven years had not changed the price of the picture ; he remembered the exact terms of our agreement and kept to them although the prices of his pictures had risen considerably in the intervening period.

A little later, the same jetty at La Croisette (on the way from Bonnard's house to ours) was treated quite differently (p. 133). The jetty itself, now even further off-centre, is seen diagonally, softened by curves and shadows. This time it is caught in the full blaze of the Mediterranean sun, represented by dazzling areas of white. Bonnard was nearly eighty when he achieved this transmutation of reality. In 1923, after he had moved to the south for the sake of his wife's health, he had made this paradoxical remark : 'I can't paint here, there are no colours.' And yet, on a visit to Henri Manguin, as long ago as 1909, he had painted the splendid *View of Saint-Tropez* (p. 171) on which he later based his famous decorative work for the Morozov palace in Moscow. In this case the painter avoids an excess of light by withdrawing into the half-shadow between the house and the trees. The bright blue of the Mediterranean appears only as a narrow strip on the left. The picture is divided in the middle by a tree; he had a subtle technique of placing the subject off-centre and restoring the balance by means of colour.

THE GENESIS OF THE GOUACHE STILL-LIFE
WITH PLUM-STONES, 1932 (p. 180)

In 1930, my mother tells us, an outbreak of boils forced Bonnard to go into hospital for treatment. He had not been there three days before he was complaining of his enforced idleness. My husband suggested that he do some painting in watercolours. He answered that this would amuse him, but it was thirty years since he had done any, and he had no paints except a little box Marthe had been given at her confirmation. Arthur went at once to get what was necessary and soon returned triumphantly with the best English paints and two immaculate marten-hair brushes. Bonnard accepted with thanks, but as soon as he unwrapped the two brushes he became very angry. 'My dear fellow, I thought you had more sense than to buy this kind of thing for me ! Those brushes must have cost you the earth, and my painting won't be any better for them.' He did not calm down until his friend had taken the two offending brushes back and exchanged them for half-a-dozen perfectly ordinary ones. Then, and only then, he set to work. But the result was a great disappointment ; all one could see was a sort of brownish sauce. As Spitteler says : 'If you mix all the bright colours together, all you get is grey.' [1] Bonnard, accustomed to retouch and correct his oil-paintings, confessed that he had no gift for the 'first thoughts' that are the essence of water-colours. 'Manet can do it,' he said, 'I just don't have the gift.' Fortunately my husband had an inspiration : he brought him some gouache.

To this we owe the extraordinary series of gouaches that Bonnard painted in the last years of his life, and which are among his most original works. But this did not come easily : the next spring, at the 'Hahnloser family's private view' there were only three gouaches. These were tentative and yet audacious. I said that I should like to have one, especially since his paintings in oils had become too difficult for me. 'It isn't good enough for you,' he said, 'I'll think about it.' I knew him well enough to say no more... We met again for Christmas at La Pauline as usual, and Bonnard sang with us the carols that reminded him, he said, of his mother who came from Alsace... I made some timid reference to the gouache that

---

[1] Denn wenn man alles Bunte mischt, so gibt es nichts als grau.

I would have liked to find among my presents. 'I haven't forgotten, Hans,' he said, 'I shall think about it.' I did not get it until the following spring, two years after the first sketch. But it is one of his best gouaches, and a very characteristic example of his compositional technique. In the centre, nothing; on the left, half-a-dozen plums and the 'milk book'; on the left, two plum-stones someone has spat out on a little plate; and a number of scattered patches of colour intersected by the edge of the picture, which only someone who knew Bonnard would recognize as his English tea-pot, his little blue box with yellow spots... and an orange object I have not been able to identify. One of the charms of Bonnard's work is its enigmatic, allusive and indefinite side.

THE PROVENÇAL JUG AND THE FADED FLOWERS
c. 1931 (p. 119)

One day, writes my mother, *we brought Bonnard a luminous bouquet of garden flowers : fresh leaves, two dark lilac-coloured irises and a mass of orange or sulphur-yellow marigolds. Bonnard put them in an orange and green Provençal jug on the mantelpiece ; and against a glowing yellow background the colour combination was intensified.*

This happened on one of our customary Thursday visits. By the Saturday all was recorded on canvas, a little paler, of course. Day by day the picture lost its brilliance just as the flowers did. The delicate leaves of the irises withered and became grey ; in the end they hung, *pitifully limp, on their stem. The whole ensemble took on an increasingly symbolic quality as it became more melancholy : it was like an image of the fragility of natural things. To see them perish and almost disappear, the stalks dry up, the twigs lose their leaves, was a profound experience. We asked Bonnard what his wife's arm was doing at the top of the picture. 'Nothing at all' he answered, 'I needed something in that part of the picture. I might just as well have hung a mascot on the wall, but I put in the arm, and that's all there is to it.' This answer is a good pointer to the style of Bonnard's last years.*

This picture is the latest to find a place in our collection; Bonnard died before we could visit him again and acquire more of his work. The colour-effect produced by an object, or its place in the composition, had taken on more importance than the object itself; thus the yellow strip at the bottom of the picture is merely a band of colour projecting forward from the mantelpiece.

A few years later, Bonnard treated a similar subject, this time in the square format he liked so much (p. 118). The composition is organized in three zones of colour—blue, white and yellow—to avoid sharp intersections of surfaces conflicting with the edge of the picture. The square is divided in two vertically, and the vase is not in the centre. The flowers are indistinct and unidentifiable : did they fade like those of the *Provençal jug* or did Bonnard only replace those in front with fresh, brilliant Riviera anemones ? The mysterious arm has been replaced by an equally mysterious piece of frame.

Young Woman by Lamplight, c.1900

Landscape with Castle, 1886

185

186   Portrait of Mme Claude Terrasse, 1890   Woman with Cat, 1891

n with Black Stockings, 1893

The Lamp, 1895-1896

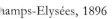

hamps-Elysées, 1896

The Bareback Rider, 1894

187

188   L'Indolente, 1899

The Family of the Composer Claude Terrasse, 1900

190   Misia and Thadée Natanson, 1902

Place Blanche, 1902

Portrait of Arï Redon, 1902

La Petite Rue, c.1903-1909

191

Portrait of Ambroise Vollard, 1906

Nude Against the Light, 1908

Paris Bridge, 1908

Marthe and her dog, Black, c.1905

Portrait of George Besson, 1911

Dining-room in the Country, 1913

In a Southern Garden, 1913

L'Estérel, c.1917

The Rape of Europa, 1919

198   Wash-stand and Mirror, 1915-1920

Rest, c.1920

Beach at Low Tide, 1920

200   The Factory, 1920

Piazza del Popolo, Rome, 1922

The Riviera, 1923

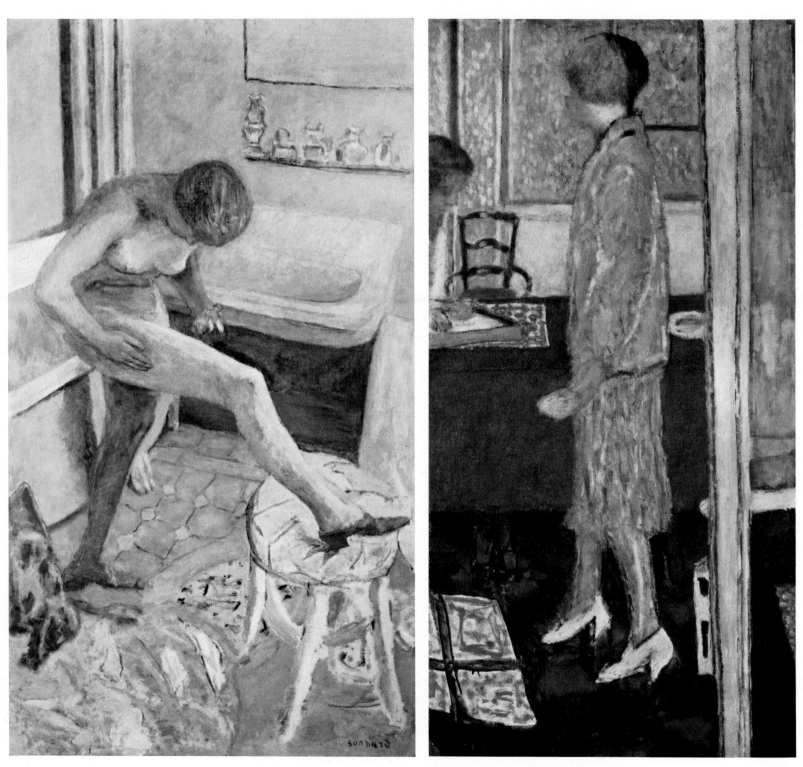

202   The Green Slipper, 1925   Standing Woman in Profile, 1923

Signac and his Friends Sailing, 1924-1925

204   Table Laid for a Meal, 1925   Reine Natanson and Marthe Bonnard, 1928

Nude with Pitcher, 1930

Two Women Standing behind a Table, c.1930

The Palm, 1926

View of Vernon, 1929

208   Breakfast, 1930-1931

Table and Garden, before 1933

White Interior, 1933

The Yellow Boat, 1936-1938

Harbour at Trouville, 1938

Yellow Nude, 1938-1940

Before Noon, 1940-1946   The Mimosa Studio, Le Cannet, 1938-1946

...rranean Landscape, 1943

The Open Window, 1945

213

Circus Horse, 1946

Almond Tree in Blossom, 1946

Illustration for L'Almanach du Père Ubu

1867   Birth of a second son, Pierre, to Eugène Bonnard, from Dauphiné, *chef de bureau* at the Ministry of War, and his wife Elise, née Mertzdorff, from Alsace; on 3 October at Fontenay-aux-Roses.

1868   Birth of Edouard Vuillard at Cuiseaux (Saone-et-Loire).

1869   Birth of Henri Matisse at Le Cateau (Nord).

1870   Birth of Maurice Denis at Granville (Manche).

1875   Death of Corot.

1877   Boarding-school, then *lycées* in Vanves and Paris (Lycée
to   Louis le Grand and Lycée Charlemagne). *Baccalauréat* and Faculty of Law.

1887   Law Degree. Starts to attend Académie Julian and Ecole des Beaux-Arts. Becomes friendly with Sérusier, Maurice Denis, Ibels, Ranson, Vallotton, Vuillard, Roussel.

1888   *Le Talisman.* The Nabis.

1889   Fails Prix de Rome and Civil Service competition. Works for assistant public prosecutor. Lives with grandmother in the Rue de Parme and rents his first studio in the Rue Le Chapelais. Sells his first poster for a hundred francs to *France-Champagne*. Commits himself to painting.

1890   Shares a little studio in the Rue Pigalle with Vuillard and Maurice Denis. Exhibition of Japanese art at the Ecole des Beaux-Arts. Death of Van Gogh. Bonnard's sister Andrée marries a young musician, Claude Terrasse.

1891   *France-Champagne* poster leads to first meeting between Lautrec and Bonnard. Bonnard exhibits at the *Salon des Indépendants* for the first time (nine pictures). First Nabi exhibition at the Galerie Le Barc de Bouteville. *La Revue Blanche*, first thought of during a holiday in Spa and first published in Liège in 1889, moves to Paris.

1892   Two pictures exhibited in the *Salon des Indépendants*, two in a group exhibition at the Galerie Le Barc de Boutteville, and one at Saint-Germain-en-Laye. Noticed by Gustave Geffroy and Roger-Marx.

1893   Studio in the Rue de Douai. Illustrates *Petites Scènes familières* and *Le Petit Solfège* by Claude Terrasse. Maurice Denis introduces him to Vollard. Maillol visits the Nabis.

215

1894 Exhibition at Galerie Le Barc de Boutteville. Lithographs a poster for *La Revue Blanche*. Meets Maria Boursin: Marthe.

1895 Vollard shows more than a hundred Cézannes, which make a deep impression on the Nabis. Publication of Bonnard's *Aspects of Paris Life*.

1896 First one-man exhibition at Galerie Durand-Ruel: fifty works (paintings, posters, lithographs). Illustrates *Marie* by Peter Nansen, published in *La Revue Blanche*. *Théâtre des Pantins* in the Rue Ballu. *Ubu Roi* at the Maison de l'Œuvre. Last exhibition at Galerie Le Barc de Boutteville to include work by the Nabis. Death of Verlaine.

1897 Sérusier's new artistic precepts alienate Bonnard, who does not believe in an art governed by mathematical laws. Group exhibition at Galerie Vollard. Colour prints for Vollard's series of albums of engravings by painters.

1898 *Marie* appears in book form. Bonnard makes the marionettes for Franc-Nohain's *Vive la France !* which is banned by the censors. Nabi exhibition at Galerie Vollard.

1899 Major group exhibition at Galerie Durand-Ruel as a 'Tribute to Redon'. Death of Sisley.

1900 Group exhibition at Galerie Bernheim-Jeune, Rue Laffitte. Vollard publishes Verlaine's *Parallèlement* illustrated by Bonnard.

1901 Denis exhibits his *Tribute to Cézanne* at the Nationale. Death of Lautrec. First Picasso exhibition at Galerie Vollard.

1902 *Daphnis et Chloé* published by Vollard. Redon paints a portrait of Bonnard, and Bonnard paints little Arï Redon. Group exhibition at the Galerie Bernheim-Jeune. Bonnard exhibits a bronze centrepiece at Galerie Vollard.

1903 15 April : last issue of *La Revue Blanche*. 8 May : death of Gauguin at Atuana. Bonnard exhibits his *Portrait of Claude Terrasse* at the *Salon des Indépendants*. Has three pictures in the first *Salon d'Automne*, including *L'Après-midi bourgeoise*. Participates in a collective exhibition at the Galerie Druet, Rue du Faubourg Saint-Honoré.

1904 Three pictures in the *Salon des Indépendants* and seven in the *Salon d'Automne*. Is represented in *La Libre Esthétique* exhibition of Impressionists in Brussels. Jules Renard's *Histoires naturelles* reprinted by Flammarion with illustrations by Bonnard. First Matisse exhibition at Galerie Vollard.

1905 Gide notices Bonnard's work at *Salon d'Automne*. Louis Vauxcelles coins the term *Fauve*.

1906 Exhibits paintings at *Salon des Indépendants, Salon d'Automne* and the Sezession in Berlin. First one-man exhibition at Galerie Bernheim-Jeune. The Académie Ranson is founded. Death of Cézanne.

1907 Group exhibition at Galerie Bernheim-Jeune. *Salon d'Automne*. Sends two paintings to an exhibition of French Impressionists in Prague. Short visits to Belgium, Holland and Germany.

1908 Illustrates Mirbeau's *La 628 E 8*. *Salon d'Automne*. Sale of the first Thadée Natanson collection including nineteen Bonnards.

1909 Paints a portrait of George Besson. Death of Paul Ranson.

1910 Discovers the south of France. One-man exhibition at Galerie Bernheim-Jeune (thirty-four paintings). First Rouault exhibition at Galerie Druet.

1911 One-man exhibition at Galerie Bernheim-Jeune, including the three panels entitled *Méditerranée*.

1912 Buys a small house, Ma Roulotte, near Vernon. Together with Vuillard, Roussel and Vallotton, Bonnard refuses the Légion d'Honneur. His studio in Paris is now at 22 Rue Tourlaque.

1913 Sends seven pictures to the Kunsthaus in Zurich. One-man exhibition at Galerie Bernheim-Jeune. Visits Holland and England in company with Vuillard.

1914 Sends five pictures to an exhibition of nineteenth-century French art in Copenhagen. Sale of Roger-Marx collection including four early Bonnards. Outbreak of war.

1915 He 'goes back to school'. Many drawings.

1916 Death of Odilon Redon. Five paintings by Bonnard presented in the exhibition of French art at Winterthur.

1917 Eleven recent works exhibited at Galerie Bernheim-Jeune.

1918 Renoir and Bonnard elected honorary presidents of the *Jeune Peinture française* group. Armistice.

1919 Death of Renoir. Léon Werth publishes the first book on Bonnard. Takes Paris flat at 56 Rue Molitor.

1920 Sends one picture to *Salon des Indépendants*.

1921 Shows twenty-four paintings at Galerie Bernheim-Jeune. Visits Rome.

1922 Exhibits at Venice Biennale.

1923 Vollard prints Mirbeau's *Dingo* with illustrations by Bonnard (published in 1927). Death of Claude Terrasse.

1924 Big retrospective exhibition at Galerie Druet, Rue Royale : sixty-eight pictures ranging from *Young Lady with Cat* (1891) to *Vase of Poppies* (1922).

1925 Buys a small villa, Le Bosquet, at Le Cannet. Paris address (his last) : 48 Boulevard des Batignolles. Still has his studio in the Rue Tourlaque. He marries Marthe. Death of Félix Vallotton.

1926 Invited to the United States to act as a member of the Carnegie Prize jury. Exhibition at the Galerie Bernheim-Jeune : twenty recent paintings. Death of Claude Monet.

1927 Charles Terrasse, Bonnard's nephew, publishes an important book on his uncle (Floury, Paris). *Dingo* is finally published. Death of Sérusier.

1928 De Hauke Gallery, New York : exhibition of forty paintings.

1929 Palais des Beaux-Arts, Brussels : Exhibition of French art including work by Bonnard.

1930 Sends seven pictures to the "painting in Paris" exhibition at the Museum of Modern Art, New York. Vollard publishes his own *Vie de Sainte Monique*, illustrated by Bonnard.

1931-32 Spends some time at Arcachon.

1932 Big Bonnard-Vuillard exhibition at the Kunsthaus in Zurich. From 1932 to 1938 Bonnard makes repeated visits to Deauville and Trouville.

1933 One-man exhibition at the Galerie Bernheim-Jeune in June, simultaneous with an exhibition of forty portraits at Galerie Braun.

1934 Shows forty-four paintings at the Wildenstein Gallery, New York.

1935 Exhibitions in Brussels, London, Boston and Paris (Galerie Braun).

1936 Awarded the second Carnegie Prize. Is represented in the exhibition 'The Painters of *La Revue Blanche*' organized by Bolette Natanson at 174 Faubourg Saint-Honoré. He also shows nineteen pictures at a Bonnard-Vuillard exhibition at the Galerie Paul Rosenberg, Rue La Boétie.

1937 Well represented in the 'Masters of Independent Art' exhibition at the Paris International Exhibition.

1938 Exhibitions in Paris (Durand-Ruel) and London. In December 1938 and January 1939 there is a Bonnard-Vuillard exhibition at the Art Institute of Chicago.

1939 Joins Laprade and Bouche in exhibitions in Paris (Durand-Ruel), Amsterdam and Stockholm. In June, exhibition of forty pastels by Bonnard and Van Dongen at Galerie Rodrigues-Henriques, Rue Bonaparte. War. Bonnard remains at Le Cannet for the duration. Death of Vollard.

1940 Pétain's armistice. Death of Vuillard.

1941 Exhibition of twelve Bonnards at the Galerie Pétridès. Sale of part of the Fénéon collection. Six of Bonnard's paintings fetch a total of one million francs.

1942 26 January : death of Marthe Bonnard at Le Cannet.

1943 Death of Maurice Denis.

1944 Liberation of France. Pierre Berès puts on an exhibition of Bonnard's graphic work in Paris. Death of Maillol and Roussel.

1945 Bonnard makes brief visit to Paris. Exhibition of forty gouaches, pastels, water-colours and drawings by Bonnard and Marquet at Galerie Rodrigues-Henriques.

1946 Visits Paris and Fontainebleau. Exhibition of thirty-four major works at Galerie Bernheim-Jeune. Twelve pictures at the *Salon d'Automne*. Bonnard approves plans for a big retrospective at the Museum of Modern Art, New York, to celebrate his eightieth birthday, but his strength is exhausted.

1947 Pierre Bonnard dies on 23 January in his little house at Le Cannet.

ILLUSTRATED BOOKS

Claude Terrasse *Petites scènes familières*, Fromont, Paris 1893.

Claude Terrasse *Le Petit Solfège*, Imprimeries Réunies, Paris 1893.

Peter Nansen *Marie*, Éditions de *La Revue Blanche*, Paris 1898.

Alfred Jarry *Petit Almanach du Père Ubu*, Paris 1899.

Paul Verlaine *Parallèlement*, Ambroise Vollard, Paris 1900.

Alfred Jarry *Grand Almanach du Père Ubu* (XXᵉ siècle), Vollard, Paris 1901.

Longus *Daphnis et Chloé*, Ambroise Vollard, Paris 1902.

Jules Renard *Histoires naturelles*, Flammarion, Paris 1904.

Octave Mirbeau *La 628 E 8*, Eugène Fasquelle, Paris 1908.

Victor Barrucand *D'un Pays plus beau*, Floury, Paris 1910.

André Gide *Prométhée mal enchaîné*, N. R. F., Paris 1920.

Claude Anet *Notes sur l'Amour*, Crès, Paris 1922.

Léopold Chauveau *Histoire du Poisson scie et du Poisson marteau*, Payot, Paris 1923.

Octave Mirbeau *Dingo*, Ambroise Vollard, Paris 1923-1927.

Léopold Chauveau *Histoires du Petit Renaud*, N. R. F., Paris 1927.

Claude Roger-Marx *Simili*, Au Sans Pareil, Paris 1930.

Ambroise Vollard *La Vie de Sainte-Monique*, Vollard, Paris 1930.

Pierre Bonnard *Correspondances*, Verve, Tériade, Paris 1944.

Pierre Louys *Le Crépuscule des Nymphes*, Pierre Tisné, Paris 1946.

Colette *Belles Saisons*, Club des lecteurs de *La Gazette des Lettres*, Paris 1947.

Couleur de Bonnard, Verve, Tériade, Paris 1947.

In about 1897 Bonnard did 144 pencil and brush drawings in the margins of a copy of La Fontaine's *Fables* on hand-made paper. This delicious work, formerly in the Barthou library, is now in the possession of André Dunoyer de Segonzac.

Above : pen drawing for Correspondances
Page 219 : Lithograph for Le Crépuscule des Nymphes
Page 220 : Sketch for Prométhée mal enchaîné, brush drawing
Pages 221-4 : Four pages from Parallèlement, lithographs

219

Bonnard

Mignonne, allons voir si ton lit
A toujours sous le rideau rouge
L'oreiller sorcier qui tant bouge
Et les draps fous. O vers ton lit!

Je te veux trop rieuse
Et très impérieuse,
Méchante & mauvaise &
Pire s'il te plaisait,
Mais si luxurieuse!

Ah, ton corps noir & rose.
Et clair de lune! Ah, pose
Ton coude sur mon cœur.
Et tout ton corps vainqueur,
Tout ton corps que j'adore!

Ah, ton corps, qu'il repose
Sur mon âme morose
Et l'étouffe s'il peut,
Si ton caprice veut!
Encore, encore, encore!

Splendides, glorieuses,
Bellement furieuses
Dans leurs jeunes ébats,
Fous mon orgueil en bas
Sous tes fesses joyeuses!

Ne fronce plus ces sourcils-ci,
Casta, ni cette bouche-ci,
Laisse-moi puiser tous tes baumes,
Piana, sucrés, salés, poivrés,
Et laisse-moi boire, poivrés,
Salés, sucrés, tes sacrés baumes.

LIST OF ILLUSTRATIONS

87
The Open Door, 1914-1920
Oil, 135×110.5 cm
Inscr. t.l. : Bonnard
Private collection, France

89
Nude washing her Foot in the Bath,
1910-1922
Oil, 106×87.5 cm
Inscr. b. centre : Bonnard
Private collection, Germany

90
Self-portrait with Beard, 1920-1925
Oil, 28×44.5 cm
Inscr. t.r. : Bonnard
Private collection, USA

91
Standing Nude, 1922-1930
Oil, 125×64 cm
Inscr. b.r. : Bonnard
Collection Mr and Mrs John D. Rocke-
feller III, USA

93
Woman in an Interior, 1925
Oil, 104×90 cm
Inscr. b. centre : Bonnard
Collection R.T., France

95
Woman at Wash-Stand, 1925
Oil, 98×55 cm
Inscr. b.r. : Bonnard
Private collection, Switzerland

105
The Sea Trip (The Hahnloser Family),
1924-1925
Oil, 98×103 cm
Inscr. b.r. : Bonnard
Formerly collection Hahnloser-Bühler,
Winterthur

107
The Harbour at Cannes, 1926
Oil, 45×63.5 cm
Inscr. b.r. : Bonnard
Collection Wildenstein Inc., USA

108
The Saucepans, 1930
Gouache, 32.5×50 cm
Inscr. b.r. : Bonnard
Formerly collection Hahnloser-Bühler,
Winterthur

114
The Mole at Saint-Tropez, 1912
Oil, 29×39 cm
Inscr. b.l. : Bonnard
Collection F. S., Switzerland

117
The Seine, 1928-1930
Oil, 39.5×56.5 cm
Inscr. b.r. : Bonnard
Private collection, USA

118
Vase of Anemones and Empty Vases,
c.1933
Oil, 63.5×69 cm
Inscr. b.l. : Bonnard
Collection F. S., Switzerland

119
Provençal Jug with Flowers, c.1931
Oil, 75.5×62 cm
Inscr. b.l. : Bonnard
Formerly collection Hahnloser-Bühler,
Winterthur

121
Basket of Fruit, 1928-1930
Oil, 39.5×44.5 cm
Inscr. b.r. : Bonnard
Collection M.C.R.O. de A., Venezuela

123
The Bathtub, 1935
Oil, 92×144 cm
Inscr. b.l. : Bonnard
Collection E.J.R., USA

127
Nude Crouching in Bathtub, 1935
Oil, 65×80.5 cm
Inscr. b.l. : Bonnard
Collection E.J.R., USA

128
Nude with Horsehair Glove, 1939
Oil, 129.5×57 cm
Inscr. t.l. : Bonnard
Private collection, USA

129
Nude in Bathtub, 1935
Oil, 103×64 cm
Inscr. b.l. : Bonnard
Collection R. T., France

131
The Jetty, c.1934
Oil, 43×56.5 cm
Inscr. b.r. : Bonnard
Formerly collection Hahnloser-Bühler,
Winterthur

133
The Jetty, 1938-1939
Oil, 38×46 cm
Inscr. b.r. : Bonnard
Collection J. W., USA

137
Self-portrait, 1939-1942
Oil, 77×62 cm
Inscr. b.r. : Bonnard
Collection Wildenstein Inc., USA

139
The Terraces, 1941
Oil, 67×72 cm
Inscr. b.r. : Bonnard
Collection C. T., France

141
View of Roofs at Le Cannet, 1941-1942
Oil, 78×100 cm
Inscr. b.l. : Bonnard
Private collection, USA

143
Peaches and Grapes, 1943
Oil, 74×46 cm
Inscr. b.r. : Bonnard
Collection D. W., USA

145
Garden in the South of France, 1943
Oil, 66.5×55.5 cm
Inscr. b.l. : Bonnard
Private collection, USA

149
Landscape on the Côte d'Azur, 1943
Oil, 26×27 cm
Inscr. b.r. : Bonnard
Collection G. Weisweiller, France

151
The Ox and the Child, 1945
Oil, 93×117 cm
Inscr. b.r. : Bonnard
Private collection, USA

159
Red Roofs at Le Cannet, 1942
Oil, 54×93.5 cm
Inscr. b.r. : Bonnard
Collection L. F., Great Britain

161
Last Self-portrait, 1944-1945
Oil, 65×47 cm
Inscr. t.l. : Bonnard
Collection C. T., France

BLACK AND WHITE PLATES *All the works reproduced on pages 167-180 were formerly in the Hahnloser-Bühler collection, Winterthur*

167
Ice-Rink, 1897-1898
Oil, 100×75 cm
Inscr. t.r. : Bonnard

168
Fiacre, *c*.1895
Oil, 25×22 cm
Inscr. b.r. : Bonnard

Woman and Children, *c*.1894
Oil, 27×18 cm
Unsigned

169
Red Garters, *c*.1906
Oil, 52.3×60 cm
Inscr. b.r. : Bonnard

The Family of Claude Terrasse,
1908-1909
Oil, 47×61 cm
Inscr. t.r. : Bonnard

170
The Red Check Tablecloth
(Marthe Bonnard and her dog),
1910-1911 Oil, 83×85 cm
Inscr. b.l. : Bonnard

The Haystack (Marthe Bonnard and a
friend), 1915-1916
Oil, 65×77 cm
Inscr. b.l. : Bonnard

171
View of Saint-Tropez, 1909-1910
Oil, 53.5×63 cm
Inscr. b.r. : Bonnard

The Seine at Vernon, 1911
Oil, 39×43 cm
Inscr. b.r. : Bonnard

171
Le Cannet from La Maison Rose, 1926
Oil, 40×55 cm
Inscr. b.r. : Bonnard
Garden near Toulon, 1915
Oil, 51×57 cm
Inscr. b.l. : Bonnard

172
Small Nude Leaning Forward, *c*.1918
Oil, 48×41 cm
Inscr. b.l. : Bonnard

The White Dress (Marthe Bonnard),
1912
Oil, 59×44 cm
Inscr. b.l. : Bonnard

Woman Undoing her Chemise, *c*.1910
Oil, 61×51.5 cm
Inscr. t.l. : Bonnard

Red Garters, *c*.1906
Oil, 61×50 cm
Inscr. b.l. : Bonnard

173
Nude by Lamplight, *c*.1912
Oil, 75.5×75 cm
Inscr. t.l.: Bonnard

174
Bouillabaisse, *c*.1910
Oil, 63×31 cm
Inscr. b.l. : Bonnard

Fruit-dish with Oranges, 1912
Oil, 68×45.5 cm
Inscr. b. centre : Bonnard

175
Table-napkins, *c*.1908
Oil, 41.5×55 cm
Inscr. b.r. : Bonnard

175
Still-life with Figure, 1912
Oil, 41×71 cm
Inscr. b.r. : Bonnard

176
Interior with the dog, Flac, 1912
Oil, 63.5×83.5 cm
Inscr. t. towards r. : Bonnard

Flowers from the South, 1914
Oil, 36×45 cm
Inscr. t.l.: Bonnard 1914

Still-life with Apples, 1924
Oil, 32×48.5 cm
Inscr. b.r. : Bonnard

177
Peaches and Grapes by Lamplight, 1919
Oil, 36.5×47 cm
Inscr. b.r. : Bonnard

Sweet Peas, *c*.1910-1912
Oil, 51×77.5 cm
Inscr. b.r. : Bonnard

178
The Sea Trip, 1924
First version in blue and white
Oil, 66×71 cm
Inscr. b.r. : Bonnard

179
Mme Hahnloser and her Skye Terrier,
1924
Sketch for *The Sea Trip*, first version
Drawing in blue pencil, 19×13.7 cm

Dr Arthur Hahnloser, 1924
Sketch for *The Sea Trip*, first version
Drawing, 16.4×12.5 cm

179
Twilight, before 1914
Oil, 128×146 cm
Inscr. b.l. : Bonnard

180
Stormy Landscape, c.1909
Oil, 49.5×65 cm
Inscr. b.l. : Bonnard

Still-life with Plum-stones, 1932
Gouache, 25.5×32.5 cm
Inscr. b.r. : Bonnard

185
Young Woman by Lamplight, c.1900
Oil, 61.5×75 cm
Inscr. b.l. : Bonnard
Kunstmuseum, Berne

Landscape with Castle, 1886
Oil, 21.5×26.5 cm
Inscr. b.l. : Bonnard
Private collection

186
Portrait of Mme Claude Terrasse, 1890
Oil, 187×80 cm
Inscr. t.r. : Bonnard 1890
Collection André Terrasse, Paris

Woman with Cat, 1891
Oil, 64×26 cm
Inscr. b.r. : PB
Private collection, Paris

187
Woman with Black Stockings, 1893
Oil, 25×33 cm
Inscr. b.l. : Bonnard 93
Private collection, Paris

The Lamp, 1895-1896
Oil, 55×71 cm
Inscr. b.l. : Bonnard
Museum of Art, Melbourne

Les Champs-Elysées, 1896
Oil, 52×76 cm
Inscr. b.l. : Bonnard
Private collection, Lausanne

The Bareback Rider, 1894
Oil, 26×35 cm
Inscr. b.r. : Bonnard 94
Formerly Bernheim-Jeune collection,
Paris

188
L'Indolente, 1899
Oil, 99×105 cm
Inscr. b.l. : Bonnard
Musée National d'Art Moderne, Paris

189
The Family of the Composer
Claude Terrasse, 1900
Oil, 139×212 cm
Inscr. b.l. : Bonnard
Collection Bernheim-Jeune, Paris

190
Misia and Thadée Natanson, 1902
Oil, 130×86 cm
Inscr. b.r. : Bonnard
Musées Royaux des Beaux-Arts, Brussels

191
Place Blanche, 1902
Oil, 60×80 cm
Inscr. b.l. : Bonnard
Collection Edward G. Robinson,
Los Angeles

Portrait of Arï Redon, 1902
Oil, 81×65 cm
Inscr. b.r. : Bonnard
Collection A. Redon, Paris

La Petite Rue, c.1903-1909
Oil, 31×22 cm
Inscr. b.r. : Bonnard
Private collection, Paris

192
Portrait of Ambroise Vollard, 1906
Oil, 74×92.5 cm
Inscr. b.r. : Bonnard
Kunsthaus, Zurich

Nude Against the Light, 1908
Oil, 125×109 cm
Inscr. b. centre : Bonnard
Musées Royaux des Beaux-Arts, Brussels

193
Paris Bridge, 1908
Oil, 74×92 cm
Inscr. b.l. : Bonnard
Collection Mr Sidney F. Brody,
Los Angeles

194
Portrait of Edouard Vuillard, c.1908
Oil, 45×37 cm
Inscr. t.l. : Bonnard
Private collection, Paris

Marthe and her dog, Black, c.1905
Oil, 70×58 cm
Unsigned
Private collection, Paris

Portrait of George Besson, 1911
Oil, 75×53 cm
Inscr. t.r. : Bonnard
Presented by Besson to the Louvre, 1965

195
Dining-room in the Country, 1913
Oil, 200×163 cm
Inscr. b.r. : Bonnard 1913
The Minneapolis Institute of Arts

196
In a Southern Garden, 1913
Oil, 84×113 cm
Inscr. b.l. : Bonnard
Kunstmuseum, Berne

L'Estérel, c.1917
Oil, 56×72 cm
Inscr. b.r. : Bonnard
Stedelijk Museum, Amsterdam

197
The Rape of Europa, 1919
Oil, 117×154 cm
Inscr. b.l. : Bonnard
The Toledo Museum of Art,
Gift of Edward Drummond Libbey, 1930

198
Wash-stand and Mirror, 1915-1920
Oil, 124×110 cm
Inscr. t.r. : Bonnard
Coll. Mr and Mrs Gustave M. Berne,
New York

199
Rest, c.1920
Oil, 56×61 cm
Inscr. t.r. : Bonnard
Collection Mme Henri Kapferer,
Boulogne-sur-Seine

Beach at Low Tide, 1920
Oil, 45×53 cm
Inscr. b.l. : Bonnard
Musée National d'Art Moderne, Paris

200
The Factory, 1920
Oil, 242×335 cm
Inscr. b.l. : Bonnard
Private collection, France

201
Piazza del Popolo, Rome, 1922
Oil, 76×96.5 cm
Inscr. b.l. : Bonnard
The Phillips Collection, Washington, D.C.

The Riviera, 1923
Oil, 79×76 cm
Inscr. b.t. : Bonnard
The Phillips Collection, Washington, D.C.

202
The Green Slipper, 1925
Oil, 142×81 cm
Inscr. b.r. : Bonnard
Collection Mr and Mrs Leigh B. Block,
Chicago

Standing Woman in Profile, 1923
Oil, 110×58 cm
Inscr. b.l. : Bonnard
Private collection, Paris

203
Signac and his Friends Sailing, 1924-1925
Oil, 124×139 cm
Inscr. b.r. : Bonnard
Kunsthaus, Zurich

204
Table Laid for a Meal, 1925
Oil, 56×38 cm
Inscr. b.r. : Bonnard
Tate Gallery, London

Reine Natanson and Marthe Bonnard,
1928
Oil, 73×57 cm
Inscr. b.r. : Bonnard
Musée National d'Art Moderne, Paris

205
Nude with Pitcher, 1930
Oil, 113×80.5 cm
Inscr. b.r. : Bonnard
Collection Bowers, France

206
Two Women Standing behind a Table,
1930
Oil, 126×95 cm
Inscr. b.r. : Bonnard
Private collection, Paris

207
The Palm, 1926
Oil, 112×146 cm
Inscr. b.r. : Bonnard 26
The Phillips Collection, Washington, D.C.

View of Vernon, 1929
Oil, 107×128 cm
Inscr. b. centre : Bonnard
Collection Mr and Mrs Alex M. Lewyt,
New York

208
Breakfast, 1930-1931
Oil, 160×113 cm
Inscr. b.r. : Bonnard
The Museum of Modern Art, New York

209
Table and Garden, before 1933
Oil, 127×135 cm
Inscr. b.l. : Bonnard
The Solomon R. Guggenheim Museum,
New York

White Interior, 1933
Oil, 109×156 cm
Inscr. b.r. : Bonnard
Musée de Grenoble

210
The Yellow Boat, 1936-1938
Oil, 58×75 cm
Inscr. b.l. : Bonnard
Collection Mr and Mrs Charles Zadock,
New York

The Harbour at Trouville, 1938
Oil, 77×103 cm
Inscr. b.l. : Bonnard
Musée National d'Art Moderne, Paris

211
Yellow Nude, 1938-1940
Oil, 170×106 cm
Inscr. b.r. : Bonnard
Private collection, New York

212
Before Noon, 1940-1946
Oil, 126×105 cm
Inscr. b.r. : Bonnard
Collection Bowers, France

The Mimosa Studio, Le Cannet,
1938-1946
Oil, 126×126 cm
Collection Charles Terrasse, Paris

213
Mediterranean Landscape, 1943
Oil, 96×72 cm
Inscr. b.l. : Bonnard
The Lazarus Phillips Family Collection,
Montreal

The Open Window, 1945
Watercolour, 65×50 cm
Unsigned
Private collection, Neuchâtel

214
Circus Horse, 1946
Oil, 94×118 cm
Inscr. b.r. : Bonnard
Collection Charles Terrasse, Paris

Almond Tree in Blossom, 1946
Oil, 55×37 cm
Unsigned
Musée National d'Art Moderne, Paris

ACKNOWLEDGEMENTS

BLACK AND WHITE PHOTOGRAPHS:

Galerie Bernheim-Jeune, Paris; James R. Dunlop, Washington: Walter Dräyer, Zurich; The Solomon R. Guggenheim Museum, New York; Martin Hesse, Berne; Raymond Laniepce, Paris; Musées royaux des Beaux-arts de Belgique; Service de documentation photographique des Musées nationaux, Versailles; Kunsthaus, Zurich; Minneapolis Institute of Arts; Kunstmuseum, Berne; Gemeente Musea van Amsterdam; Toledo Museum of Arts; André Ostier, Paris; Studio Picardy, Grenoble; Phillips Collection, Washington; Photo Routhier, Paris; Soichi Sunami, Museum of Modern Art, New York; Sam Salz Inc., New York; Jacques Salomon, Paris; Tate Gallery, London; Wildenstein Inc., New York.

COLOUR PHOTOGRAPHS:

Walter Dräyer, Zürich; Paul Schori, Berne; Wildenstein Inc., New York.

Book designed by André Rosselet, Neuchâtel. Printed in Switzerland by Paul Attinger S.A., Neuchâtel. Colour offset films and blocks made by Schwitter S.A., Basel, Zürich, Lausanne. Line blocks engraved by Clichés Rapid, Yverdon.

Printed in Switzerland.